Gone Surfing

The Golden Years of Surfing in New Zealand, 1950-1970

Penguin Books

Contents

Dawn

The first surfers in New Zealand **6**
Surfing in the 1950s **6**
Progress is made 7
In Wellington 9
In Christchurch 10
In Hamilton 11
And in Dunedin 12
A view from the outside 12
Where to from here? 12

First Wave

There were other explorers **15**
Finding the faithful **17**
At first, in Auckland 18
Meanwhile, in Wellington 18
And in Hamilton 19
While, in Christchurch 20
And finally, in Dunedin 20
The swell picks up **21**
New Zealand's first alternative culture? **21**
Who rules the beaches? **22**
New recruits 24
An industry is born **24**
South of the Bombay Hills 28
And the rest made do 31
Just surfing **33**
Kick out **36**

Second Wave

The arrival of competitive surfing **38**
'Hermit' 40
Word gets out – visitors come in **40**
Watch out ... the Aussies are coming! 43
The new board builders **46**
Atlas Woods Surfboards 46
Peter Way 51
Frank Wilkin 51
Roger Land 52
Rodney Davidson 53

Ted Davidson 54
Ken Clark 55
Dave Jackman 56
And the rest 59
From First Wave to Second Wave **60**
Peter Byers 60
Peter Miller 60
Denis Quane 60
What about the surfers? **61**
Meanwhile, at the beach **61**
'We will fight them on the beaches ...' 61
To go where no other has **63**
And the weather today 68
Discovering the lost tribes 70
Falling off the edge of the earth 76
It's not about winning or losing **79**
Girls can do anything **84**
The paraphernalia **91**
Lights, camera, action! 91
Making the scene with a magazine 92
Surf music 93
Surf clothing 94

Third Wave

Talkin' 'bout a revolution **96**
Disillusionment with competition **98**
Who was the winner on the day? 98
Interclub competition 102
Windansea 102
But wait, there's more 104
First to see the light? **105**
The Wild West **110**
Wellington has waves? **112**
And on the mainland **113**
Riding into the next decade **114**

Close out **116**

Epilogue **117**

Glossary/Bibliography **126**

Profiles

Peter Byers **25**

Bob Davie **47**

Denis Quane **57**

DEL Surfboards **65**
Dave Littlejohn **65**
Nigel Dwyer **66**

Mr President **77**
Dave Walpole **77**
Peter Fitzsimmons **78**

Peter Way **81**

Roger Land **89**

Wayne Parkes **99**

Alan Byrne **107**

Foreword – Gary McCormick

The joy of surfing lies in its innocence. One man/one woman – one wave!

Its relative simplicity is what separates surfing out from other sports. The sea is a cleansing agent (producing clouds of negative ions, which revitalise us) washing the tension and tedium of day-to-day life away.

I started surfing on a wooden board before saving up money from my paper round to buy an old Malibu board. Titahi Bay, north-west of Wellington, produced the kind of big, hairy onshore surf which made you appreciate the sea in all its moods.

I will never forget the first couple of rides – surging forward on a wave! It was such a wild idea.

Nor should you forget, if you have had the good fortune to experience it. It will be the defining moment of your life. Even if you succumb to the pressures of a family or career and drift away from surfing, it will come back to haunt you. You will either curse the fact that you left it behind, or take it up again.

In the early days, surfers were regarded as 'bums', spoken of in the same manner as 'bikies'. We looked to California then and David Nuuhiwa's ten second nose ride. Then Nat Young and the Australian 'animals' took over. The cosmic rides of the sixties and early seventies gave way to the growing prize money of the eighties. Surfing has now entered the mainstream and is starting to look like a truly professional sport.

'Only through the act of wave-riding can wave-riding be known', wrote one of the sages of the Aussie *Surf International* magazine back in the age of Captain Goodvibes. Such a simple truth.

In the end, it is a matter of one man or woman – and the sea. Competitions, professionalism and trophies are mere icing on someone else's cake. The act of riding a wave burns a special kind of consciousness into the human soul. It remains changed for a lifetime.

Pick up your board and walk!

Gary McCormick

Foreword – Luke Williamson

The motivation behind this book was the desire to collect the memories and images of the pioneers of surfing before they were lost forever. I was inspired by the surf history articles that appeared in *The Surfer's Journal,* from California.

Having now spent two years gathering the material for this book, I feel enriched by the people I have met and the knowledge I have gained. The process has only served to convince me that this book was a worthwhile exercise.

To the many who have asked why I stopped at 1970, the answer is that from that point on there were many magazines and images that recorded the state of surfing, and I didn't feel there was such a danger of the information going unrecorded. Also, there were so many surfers by then that the history became a description of trend and design rather than individual tales. Lastly, the so-called 'soul' of surfing in the sixties is what current surfers are looking to emulate in board and style, and that was what needed to be accurately (I hope) assembled.

I apologise to the hundreds of worthy surfers from the sixties to whom I was unable to talk. I hope that you will contact me with your stories with the view to a possible second edition of this book. If you are wondering who was interviewed for the book, I refer you to the list of thank yous on page 128.

I also apologise for any inaccuracies in the book. I was questioned at one stage as to whether I could guarantee the authenticity of the material herein - I can guarantee the authenticity of the people to whom I spoke but not the material. Forty-year-old memories can be a bit uncertain and can change from one telling to the next so I have cross-referenced and checked at every possible point. The many quotes I have used in this book often relate stories that cannot be confirmed but do provide the 'flavour' of the times. Enjoy them in the spirit in which they were experienced and recounted.

I have also come to one other observation which is that despite the wayward behaviour and supposed antisocial character of surfers, to get a car, go camping for a week and take on the ocean with a surfboard requires quite a degree of organisation, self-confidence and fitness. Surfing helps create individuals who are well armed for what life has ahead.

I was surprised at how little I knew of the history of this sport that I loved so dearly, and I hope that reading this book will give everyone a pleasant surprise about 'where we come from'.

(above) **Duke Kahanamoku during his visit to New Zealand in 1915. Duke was the star of a swimming race held in the Devonport dry dock, Auckland. Several hundred people came to see the Olympic champion and witness him breaking New Zealand swimming records.**

(previous page) **'The Paddleboard Club', Mount Maunganui 1957. (l to r) Unknown, unknown, Laurie Jessup, Peter Miller, Peter 'Ripa' Edwards, 'Weasel' and John 'Brownie' Lambert.**

The first surfers in New Zealand

When Europeans arrived in New Zealand they found that coastal Maori tribes were surfing (*whakaheke ngaru*) using relatively uncrafted boards (*kopapa*), logs (*paparewa*), canoes (*waka*) and even kelp bags (*poha*). The sport was not as developed as in Hawaii but was a regular summertime activity. Some tribes in the Canterbury area were reported to have used boards that could support up to three people.

The arrival of missionaries in New Zealand in the mid- to late-1800s led to many Maori becoming Christians. Surfing was not as institutionalised in Maori society as it was in Hawaiian society but concerns for religious propriety, as well as Victorian dress codes, did permeate Maori custom and hasten the demise of distinctive Maori aquatic activities, including surfing.

New Zealand's reintroduction to surfing came with a demonstration by the Hawaiian Olympic swimming champion, Duke Kahanamoku, at Wellington's Lyall Bay in 1915. 'The Duke' was touring the world following his Olympic success and, after being in the forefront of the surfing revival in Hawaii, he took every possible opportunity to demonstrate 'the sport of the kings' in the countries he visited. For this brief preview of the surfing phenomenon that was to come The Duke used a solid wooden board, about 10 feet long, with no fin. He paddled out at Lyall Bay then rode a wave in towards shore before walking off the front of the board and body surfing to the beach. The *Auckland Weekly News* reported that he also gave a surfing demonstration at Muriwai, on Auckland's West Coast, but it is not clear what sort of board he used or whether he stood up.

His Wellington demonstration made quite an impression on the local surf life saving club members and during the 1920s a number of surfers at Maranui were using up to 16-foot solid wooden boards in the waves. However, surfing didn't really catch on as a sport and over the following years, surf life saving remained the dominant expression of water sports at the beach.

Surfing in the 1950s

During the 1950s, post-war exports meant that New Zealand was enjoying a period of relative affluence. People were enjoying more leisure time and, with the increasing availability of cars, they began to visit the beaches in greater numbers, creating a need for more surf life savers.

Surf culture in New Zealand, during this decade, was almost entirely based around the surf life saving movement. The surf life saving clubs were highly structured with an emphasis on team work, cooperation and service to the community, plus a healthy dose of competition. These characteristics of team work and duty were central to New Zealand's social makeup during the 1950s, with team sports being epitomised by the All Blacks, and the 'let's all pull together' attitude, a continuing after-effect of World War Two. Commitment to the club and team was very strong.

The surf life saving clubs provided a vital base at beaches for those who enjoyed the beach and the ocean. Like-minded people could meet one another, perform an important social service and indulge in a bit of competition if they so desired. Many young men, in particular, joined the local surf life saving clubs in order to have a place to stay at the beach. There were some baches (holiday homes) at popular beaches but they were still few and far between so the surf life saving club provided an ideal place to stay.

For those who were interested in riding the surf, the surf life saving club was also the place where suitable equipment could be found, including surf boats, surf skis and longboards. The longboard was the precursor of modern surfboards and was first developed and ridden by Tom Blake in Hawaii during the 1930s. Tom designed the board for paddleboard races and developed from there to standing up on them in the surf. Surf life saving associations recognised their potential for surf rescues and they became an essential piece of rescue equipment.

Longboards had an internal wooden frame to which ply was attached, and resembled the structure of an aircraft wing. They were given a good layer of varnish to waterproof them and were extremely heavy when finished – about 70-100 pounds. Initially the boards had no fin although design refinements towards the end of the 1950s resulted in the placement of a small fin on the back of some boards. The boards were hard to manoeuvre and would take in water during use. A bung was usually included to allow the water to be drained out and to allow air to escape if they were sitting in the sun at the beach. Because the boards were so heavy, people tended to store them at their local surf life saving club.

Surf skis were similar in design to the longboards but were made for sitting on and paddling with a canoe paddle. They were characterised in New Zealand by the 'teardrop' design which was used by most of the surf life saving clubs. Like the longboards, surf skis were very heavy, hard to manoeuvre and were infamous for injuring their riders in the surf.

Progress is made

As the 1950s progressed, more information became available on the building of longboards specifically for surf riding. Plans for building the boards began to appear in overseas magazines, some of which made it into the hands of surf life saving enthusiasts around the country.

In 1950, a member of the East End Surf Life Saving Club in New Plymouth, Colin McCoombs, came across a 1947 *Popular Mechanics* magazine in which there were plans for a Tom Blake paddleboard. He built the 12-foot board using a white pine frame, marine ply, many screws and the first lot of Aerolux glue available in New Plymouth. To say the least, Colin was excited when he stood on it and surfed in on the waves. He made quite an impression at the beach where surf skis were the norm. Colin left his board on the beach one night, believing he had pulled it up far enough to avoid the waves, only to find in the morning that it had been washed away. It was later recovered down the coast and repaired by another New Plymouth legend, Leith Beaurepaire.

In 1952, at Mount Maunganui, Ron White and Jock Carson built one of the first hollow plywood surfboards in New Zealand.

PHOTO RON WHITE

(left) Longboards had an internal wooden frame to which ply was attached and they resembled the structure of an aircraft wing. Ron White shows off the frames of the first two boards he and Jock Carson built at Mount Maunganui in 1952.

(above) **Ron White and Jimmy Carson with a hollow longboard, Mount Maunganui 1953.**

A friend of Ron's had returned from Auckland with a page ripped from *Popular Mechanics* magazine (perhaps the same copy Colin McCoombs saw), showing a plan for a Tom Blake longboard. Because Ron was a builder, his friend gave him the plan to look over. None of them had ever even seen a surfboard before, let alone built one. The board was 10'6" long, two feet wide and about four inches deep. Its makeup was similar to an aircraft wing but with a long, tapered tail and rounded nose, no rocker and square rails. Pukatea hardwood was used for the frame and nearly two sheets of quarter inch marine ply were used to cover the board. It was held together with marine glue and approximately 18 dozen three-quarter inch screws. The board was given a beautiful, if slippery, varnish finish.

It took Ron nearly three months of part-time work to finish the board and when he and Jock tried to ride it they found surfing more difficult than expected, suffering numerous slips and nose dives. They decided to experiment and built a 14' board based on the same design as the first. They found the board easier to stand on but still had trouble with slipping off and nose diving.

Jock was quickly learning the wood working skills required to make the boards and they produced a third board for Jock's brother, Jimmy Carson. Ron and Jock spent a lot of time in the water practising their new sport and both spoke fondly of those early days, sitting in the surf with no one else out, just enjoying the chance to chat and catch some waves.

Later in 1952, Ron and Jock went to Sydney on holiday and attended a surf carnival at Narrabeen. There they saw a hollow surfboard that had rocker built into it (referred to as a 'banana' board by the locals). They watched the board's performance in the waves and quickly realised that, due to this rocker, it didn't nose dive like their boards. The board also had small rails screwed onto the sides of the deck to stop the rider slipping off when paddling and surfing.

Ron White: *'Being a builder, I happened to have a tape measure with me so I took the measurements of the board and brought them back to Mount Maunganui. The measurements of the Australian board were similar in most respects to the 14-footers Jock and I had built but it had the important "banana" innovation and the rails.'*

Ron and Jock built four boards together. They added a handle to the tail of the fourth board so that a rider could hang on to it when he fell off and avoid having to swim after it so often (this board was sold to Taffy Davies). Ron then gave up building boards although he still spent time at the surf club and went out surfing when at the beach. He didn't take up surfing on the new polystyrene Malibu boards, finding them unmanageable. Work and family commitments eventually led to his dropping out of surfing.

Jock continued on, trying to refine materials and design. He acknowledges that being single allowed him the time to pursue surfboard building and surfing. Jock tried longer and shorter designs but settled on a core design of 14' with rounded sides and narrow nose. He built 10-12 of those for local surf club members. As fast as Jock could build a board, which took about 2-3 months of evening and weekend work, it would be bought by new enthusiasts, such as Neville Weal and Jim Raymond. Jock would also post plans off around the country to other surf enthusiasts who had heard about his boards, or he would give away plans at surf life saving carnivals. Barry Parkinson was a Mount local who began making boards based on Jock's plans.

Jock saw surfing as an excellent way to encourage new surf club members as it was the younger beach-goers, in particular, who were interested in surfing. The boards were stored at the club rooms and they would attract youngsters to the club.

It was noted by three of the early surfers that the big boards had a great advantage in their ability to carry two people, so young women from the beach could be paddled into the surf and dates arranged. The paddler was also afforded an excellent view of the young woman's derrière. And as one wife later pointed out, *'Even though I was terrified of the big waves, I was not going to have my place taken by one of the other girls, and risk losing my boyfriend.'*

All the rides at this stage were straight lines, either into the beach or, if you could line up the right wave and paddle in at the right angle, a line across the beach on the face of the breaking wave. However, there was little chance of changing direction once you had started. Taffy Davies: *'I still remember one ride I got from outside the blowhole at Mount Maunganui's main beach, right across the beach to the surf club, a distance of several hundred metres.'*

The increase in the number of surfers was also good news for rescue work. There were more capable people in the water and they were right on the spot when things went wrong. Jock maintains to this day that surf rescue benefited from the popularity of surfing and that drownings decreased in the 60s, despite there being more people at the beach. He viewed it as a new rescue form available outside the Surf Life Saving Association.

In all, Jock made about 25 longboards before the arrival of polystyrene in 1959-60. He didn't take up surfing on the new Malibu boards but he kept up his surf life saving work well into the 1970s.

In Wellington ...

Chas (Charles) Lake, one of the first surfers in Wellington, found plans for a Tom Blake longboard in a 1939 edition of *Popular Science* magazine, from the USA. In the early 1950s, he built himself a 14-foot longboard and painted it with yellow and black stripes. He surfed it at Maranui Beach in Wellington, where he belonged to the Maranui Surf Life Saving Club, as well as Lyall Bay and Waimarama. It was at Waimarama, a few years later, that he met Peter Miller from Hamilton. Peter was a Mount Maunganui Surf Club member and he had built a hollow longboard with similar attributes to the modern Malibu that was soon to appear. From Peter, Chas heard that there was a lot of interest in surfboards at the Mount Maunganui Surf Life Saving Club so he hitch-hiked there in 1958 to see what was going on. He found that the Mount Maunganui surf life savers, particularly Jock Carson, were building and riding 14-foot Tom

(above) This longboard, the fourth built by Ron White and Jock Carson, featured a metal handle on the tail for the rider to grab onto when he fell off, thus avoiding a long swim. This board was bought by Taffy Davies.

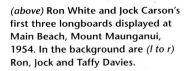

(above) Ron White and Jock Carson's first three longboards displayed at Main Beach, Mount Maunganui, 1954. In the background are (l to r) Ron, Jock and Taffy Davies.

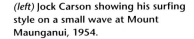

(left) Jock Carson showing his surfing style on a small wave at Mount Maunganui, 1954.

(below) Taffy Davies and willing helpers in a demonstration of how heavy the boards were.

(right) **Chas Lake riding his Tom Blake-inspired longboard at Maranui Beach, Wellington, 1956 – looking as if he is walking on water.**

(left, l to r) **Jim Mowtell, Greg Horton, 'the 16-footer', Chas Lake and Sam Crawford. Visiting Westshore Beach, Napier, 1957.**

(below, l to r) **Murray Haxton and Kerry Ansell with Chas Lake's yellow and black-striped longboard at Lyall Bay, Wellington, 1957.**

Blake designs and a longer board of around 16 feet. Chas made annual trips thereafter, to compare design ideas, and he forged a lasting bond with the Mount Maunganui Surf Life Saving Club.

In Christchurch ...

Tony Johnson of Christchurch was building longboards from the mid-1950s, based on an Australian design. His boards featured a veneer dolphin on the nose and, together with Neil Truscott, he estimates he built over 100 longboards and surf skis. Tony was a surf life saving enthusiast and never took up Malibu surfing. However, a young surf life saver who spent some time in Tony's workshop, picking up the skills for making longboards, was to become the 'king' of Malibu board building in the South Island.

Denis Quane had been experimenting with longboards and surf skis at Sumner Beach, Christchurch, since the early 1950s. By the mid-1950s, Denis was very keen on the new longboards and spent a lot of time out in the waves trying to perfect his surfing. However, Denis believed he could make a better board, so he started by building a shed in his parents' back yard. With a suitable workspace now available, he designed a surf ski, built it and won a few races (against the seniors in the surf life saving club). He followed this success by building some hollow paddleboards and won a few races with these. It was nearing the end of the 50s and Denis was enjoying his surfing and board building but was still looking to advance his surf equipment.

Denis saw his first modern Malibu board late in 1958. A local woman, Bev Breward, had been to Australia and brought back a Gordon Woods hot dog board, made with a balsa core and fibreglass coating. Around the same time, two members of the Sumner Surf Life Saving Club made a polystyrene board that no one was able to ride. They gave it to Denis who taught himself to ride it over the next year. Modern boardbuilding materials were, therefore, very much in Denis' mind when he travelled to New Plymouth, as a junior, for the 1959 national surf life saving champs ...

In Hamilton ...

In 1957, in Hamilton, Peter Miller made a longboard based on a design published in *Australian Outdoors Magazine* and it was probably the most up-to-date surfboard in the country at the time. Peter Miller: '*I built a 10' longboard, 24" wide by 4" deep, out of a hollow white pine frame screwed to redwood nose and tail blocks. This was covered with thin marine ply. The rails were rounded, shaped redwood, and the fin was wood, 12" deep, shaped and fibreglassed to the board. I remember turning up at the Mount Maunganui Surf Life Saving Club with it when I had finished. No one had seen such a short board, and had never seen rounded rails or a fin. "That fin won't last the day," shouted the club members. The board was hard to stand up on so I glued beading along the rails to stop myself from slipping off when standing – no one had told us about using wax.*'

Peter was happy with the performance of his new board and he returned to Hamilton determined to refine the design.

This was the first appearance of a true fin on a surfboard and already it was at least seven years after Malibu boards first appeared in California. All around the country, at the surf life saving clubs, surfers were using surf skis and longboards to ride the waves. There was a lot of experimentation going on in terms of board size and use of fins, as can be seen by the description of Peter Miller's 1957 longboard, but it was all in the realm of hollow ply boards. We must also remember that 'surfing', at this stage, entailed battling out through the waves, turning around and riding a breaking wave in a straight line to the beach. There was some degree of tracking across a wave ('broaching' as it was referred to) as the longboard designs improved towards the end of the 1950s but there was no ability to trim on the face of a wave. Nor was there much understanding that a wave could be effectively ridden that way.

Surf life saving was still the dominant philosophy and most of the surf activity went on in the surf life saving environment.

In California, the hothouse of surfboard design in the 1950s, surfing was able to develop as a separate sport outside the

PHOTO DENIS QUANE

(left, l to r) Des Lyons with a Tony Johnson longboard (with Tony's signature dolphin on the nose), Denis Quane with a self-built longboard and Kerry McDonald, Sumner Beach, Christchurch, 1956.

(below, l to r) Kent Pearson, Denis Quane and Kerry McDonald (complete with oilskin hat) riding their hollow longboards at Sumner Beach, Christchurch, 1962.

PHOTO DENIS QUANE

11

confines of surf life saving because the USA had a professional lifeguard service. Going to the beach and staying there to surf did not require getting involved with the surf life saving movement. Thus, while a strong counter-culture of surfers was establishing itself in California, the phenomenon had not reached New Zealand. In New Zealand, surf life saving was performed by volunteers and, outside of competition, there was little transport of surf life saving equipment around the country.

And in Dunedin ...

Bart Smaill started a lifetime of surf life saving at Dunedin's Saint Clair club in 1952. He used surf skis to begin with and then longboards as they became available. He was a keen competitor in paddleboard racing and had become interested in surfing in on the waves during his time on the longboards. He was very interested in refining longboard shapes for competitive paddleboard racing when he went to the 1959 national surf life saving champs in New Plymouth.

PHOTO PETER MILLER

(above) Peter Miller with his 1957 Malibu-inspired longboard, named 'Enid'. This was one of the first boards to have a true fin and round rails, and it was much shorter, at 10'6", than the norm of 14-16'.

(right) The size difference of 'Enid' is obvious in this photo which shows a collection of longboards at Mount Maunganui, 1957.

PHOTO PETER MILLER

PHOTO PETER MILLER

(right) A selection of boards built by Peter Miller, displayed at Mount Maunganui, 1960. (l to r) Marg with a 14' longboard, Marilyn Miller with 10'6" Enid, and Kaye with one of Peter's first polystyrene Malibu boards.

A view from the outside

Bud Browne, the legendary Californian surf film maker, visited New Zealand in 1957 after a trip to film the surf in Australia. During his three-week stay in New Zealand he visited Muriwai and filmed a surf canoe in action. He also visited other beaches such as Piha and Mount Maunganui but never saw any surfers. *'I was impressed by the surf potential in New Zealand, the beautiful scenery and the friendly people but I never saw any surfers – I would have filmed them if I had.'*

Bud brought two of his movies with him, *Surfing in Hawaii* and *Riding the Big Surf* which were shown at the Berkeley Theatre in Mission Bay to a crowd of surf life saving enthusiasts. They were reputedly unimpressed by the size of the waves, believing the West Coast to be a match. Bud returned home in April 1958 and the movies seem to have had little impact on the locals in terms of sending converts out searching for new surfboards and surf skills.

Where to from here?

So, a group of surfers was developing within the surf life saving community who were fascinated by riding waves but restricted by their equipment. They were still dedicated life savers but they had found a new way of enjoying the ocean that was more exciting. The time was ripe for a revolution in board riding.

The revolution came courtesy of two young Californians who arrived in New Zealand in the summer of 1958-59.

First wave

PHOTO PETER MILLER

PHOTO BING COPELAND

(above, l to r) Rick Stoner and Bing Copeland sporting the uniform of the Piha Surf Life Saving Club, 1959. They spent four months in New Zealand, staying at the Piha Surf Life Saving Club.

(right) Rick Stoner, in Hawaii, with the two Velzy balsa boards that he and Bing brought to New Zealand. Rick's board is on the left and Bing's is on the right.

(below) Rick Stoner and Bing Copeland in Tahiti prior to their departure for New Zealand. Their boards can be seen stowed above the cabin of the yacht in the background.

PHOTO BING COPELAND

PHOTO BING COPELAND

In November 1958, Bing Copeland and Rick Stoner, lifeguards for Los Angeles County, set off on a South Seas adventure. Bing Copeland: 'Rick and I set out, crewing on a yacht bound for Tahiti. We started in Honolulu and sailed to Tahiti where we stayed for two months, enjoying the Polynesian atmosphere. Rick and I surfed good waves at the entrance to the harbour at Moorea.

'We joined an Australian schooner and sailed on to Bora Bora, Rarotonga and Fiji. On November 27, 1958, we arrived in Auckland. We met a couple of guys and asked them if they knew of any surf near by and they offered to take us to Piha the next day.

'We got our boards off the boat and on to their car, and took the scary drive (the wrong side of the road for us) to Piha. Arriving at the surf club, we met many nice guys including Peter Byers. The waves looked good (about 5-6 feet) so we paddled out and rode eight or ten waves each, and it was fun. The surf club guys sent a few of their members out on surf skis to look after us.

'Upon returning to the beach, we were surrounded by guys wanting to "give our boards a go". I believe our boards never left the water, during the daylight hours, for the next few weeks.

'We were so well received by the Piha Surf Club members, that we decided to stay awhile and enjoy the surf and companionship. They let us to stay in the clubhouse, took us to their homes and fed us well – we certainly ate our share of Peter's stewed tomatoes with sausages (snags).

'Since we grew up helping around Velzy's surf shop in California, we thought we would try to build a few boards for the club members at Piha. We located styrofoam and epoxy resin in Auckland and, in the clubhouse, built the boards. That led to Rick and I starting our own successful surfboard businesses after returning to California.

'Everyone in New Zealand was so wonderful to us. I will be eternally grateful for the acceptance and friendships we had. I have many wonderful memories of the time we spent in your country, including the tomato fights in Peter Byers' tomato fields.

'In February of 1959, we bought passage on the Orient Line and returned to California in time to resume our lifeguarding jobs. In October of that year, we opened our first surf shop.

'It was so unfortunate and unfair that Rick Stoner should be taken from us by a brain tumour at an early age. Rick was the most generous and caring person I've had the pleasure to be associated with.'

Bing and Rick brought with them two of the first modern surfboards to be seen in New Zealand. They each had a Velzy (built by Dale Velzy of California) Malibu board made from a shaped balsa core which was covered with fibreglass mat and resin. Compared to any board in New Zealand at the time, they were lightweight (probably about 30 pounds) and manoeuvrable.

The local surf life savers, who had only experienced the hollow plywood rescue boards, were quickly captivated by the new boards and the idea of surfing across the face of a wave. Peter Byers, in particular, spent as much time as possible on the new boards and quickly became a proficient surfer and good friends with Rick and Bing.

Peter was a keen surf life saver who lived at Piha and grew tomatoes for a living. When he saw Rick and Bing surfing across the face of the waves, and doing turns, life changed radically for him. Peter became one of New Zealand's first modern surfers.

Rick and Bing built two paddleboards for the 1959 national surf life saving champs at New Plymouth, and started making five surfboards for the local club members. The paddleboards were an orange, square-tailed, 10'6" board, and a 13' thin raceboard. Both were made from shaped insulation polystyrene and covered with resin and chopped strand fibreglass. Neither Rick nor Bing had built boards before. They had, however, spent time at the Velzy factory in California and felt confident enough, with Peter's assistance, to try building the boards at Piha.

Peter drove them all over Auckland to find the necessary supplies to build the boards. This was to Peter's advantage when he came to build his own boards in the following year as he then knew what materials were needed and where to get them.

Peter, Rick and Bing went with the Piha surf life saving team to the 1959 national surf life saving championships at Oakura Beach, New Plymouth, and the new surfboards were introduced to the rest of the surf life saving community. Rick and Bing entered the paddleboard races on their lightweight Malibu boards and easily won. The new boards caused quite a stir for both their speed in paddleboard racing and for their performance in the surf.

When the competitions were over, Rick and Bing lent the boards to surf life saving competitors who were interested, to try out in the surf. The reaction was the same as when Rick and Bing first introduced the boards to Piha – they were fascinated by what the boards could do. A whole new world of surfing suddenly became possible and those national champs were the beginning of the spread of modern surfing throughout New Zealand.

Rick and Bing returned to California before they managed to finish the five surfboards they had shaped at Piha. Peter Byers bought the boards and finished them off, selling them on to locals, such as Peter Way and Murray Bray, who were keen to take up surfing.

There were other explorers

The Taranaki area produced several early board builders, of whom Dave Littlejohn may have been the earliest.

Dave Littlejohn: *'I can't remember where I first saw surfing but it was probably in a magazine. I just decided to make a board based on what I had seen so I got bits of polystyrene, stuck them together and glassed it all up. Of course it dissolved but I started again, using a protective layer between the glass and the foam, and launched my first board at East End around the summer of 1956-57. The board was a flat plank with no shape to speak of but I surfed it until the new production boards started arriving from Dunlop and Quane around 1962. I got a lot of strange looks because there was nobody*

PHOTO BING COPELAND

(above, l to r) **Rick Stoner and Bing Copeland demonstrate their skills in the waves at Piha, 1958. With their balsa and fibreglass Malibu boards, and the ability to ride across the face of waves, these two Californians suddenly awakened New Zealanders to the art and equipment of modern surfing.**
Bing Copeland: *'Upon returning to the beach, we were surrounded by guys wanting to give our boards a go. I believe our boards never left the water, during the daylight hours, for the next few weeks.'*

PHOTO DAVE LITTLEJOHN

(left) **Dave Littlejohn at Raglan, 1964.** *'I'm wearing a yellow wetsuit that Jim Mowtell sent me from Hawaii. It was the first wetsuit I had ever seen.'*

(above) **Dave Littlejohn sold this shot of Leith Beaurepaire at Waiwhakaiho to** *Surfer* **magazine. Dave Littlejohn:** *'I discovered the river mouth bar at Waiwhakaiho and had it to myself for over a year before some of the others spotted me from Fitzroy. We called it Spot X and I then had to share it with almost half a dozen other people!'*

(below) **Bob Atherton at Shipwreck Bay, Northland, 1962. Bob and his wife Joan surfed and built boards in wonderful isolation in the Far North for about three years.**

(below left) **Bob and Joan's first home-made Malibu boards, 1960-61.**

else around with a Malibu board until Peter Quinn and Leith Beaurepaire came along a couple of years later.'

21-year-old Peter Quinn of New Plymouth, discovered an Australian magazine which had a feature on making surfboards. Along with some friends, Peter made his own board and surfed it at East End, New Plymouth, December 1958. This would have been almost exactly the time that Bing and Rick were wowing the locals at Piha with modern surfing.

A travelling salesman from Epiglass, who was demonstrating the new resins while visiting New Plymouth, explained to Peter the need for a protective coat (Ados glue in this case) between resin and polystyrene. So, unlike those of many first-time builders, Peter's board didn't break in half on its first outing. He remembers the shape being rather barge-like but the board did work.

Leith Beaurepaire was a contemporary of Peter Quinn who started surfing around 1958-59 on a board he made himself. Leith got his design and instructions from a library book called *Surfing in Hawaii*. *'I made a couple of boards with Peter Quinn, then some more of my own for the locals before Atlas Woods and Dunlop boards became available.*

'As far as I can remember, I was the first surfer in New Plymouth. I surfed on my own, mainly at Fitzroy, and people would stare at me wondering what sort of board I had and what I was up to. I was soon joined by Peter Quinn, Larry Wilkie, Des Paynter and others.'

As the first surfers around New Plymouth, Dave, Leith, Peter and friends faced the problem of learning the sport in a vacuum. There was nobody to get advice or inspiration from, and it was several more years before there were visiting surfers, movies or magazines to help.

1958 seems to have been a pivotal year in the arrival of surfing in New Zealand. In Auckland and New Plymouth the first Malibu boards were appearing, and New Zealand visitors to Australia were starting to return with boards by 1959. It is almost as if a timer had gone off and it was time to surf. But there was still some work to do.

Bob Atherton and his wife Joan lived at Ahipara in the far

north of New Zealand. Bob was a butcher in the nearby town of Kaitaia. He and Joan had done some camping at Muriwai Beach and seen the original wooden belly boards, but they had never seen any sort of surfboard.

Bob saw a plan for a Malibu board in an Australian magazine (perhaps the same that Peter Quinn saw) in 1960 and thought it would be perfect for the surf that rolled in on Ninety Mile Beach. He sourced some insulation foam in Kaitaia and travelled to Auckland to get resin from Epiglass. Bob then began building his own board with only the magazine instructions to follow. It was a remarkable effort considering he had never seen surfing or a surfboard before.

Bob and Joan launched the board at Ninety Mile Beach, during the summer of 1960-61, and began learning to surf. Again without guidance or information, through trial and error, they learned how to stand up and ride the white water to the beach.

Starting in 1960, Joan was one of New Zealand's first woman surfers on the modern Malibu boards. *I only liked the small waves really but I loved to ride the nose at Wreck Bay – that was my favourite.'* Swimmers at Ninety Mile Beach were rare, so surfers, and a woman surfer at that, were unheard of. Joan also taught a number of Kaitaia locals to surf over the following years.

Bob and Joan saw no other surfers for at least two to three years. They travelled all over the far north during that time and were the first surfers at any beaches they chose to visit.

'On one visit to Tokerau Beach, we met up with Alf Locke, who we had previously met at Epiglass in Auckland. He was amazed that we had Malibu boards. Alf was only aware of other surfers at Piha but he was the one who explained that we could surf across the face of the wave rather than just straight into the beach. This was a huge revelation and improved our surfing experiences enormously.'

Finding the faithful

Attending the 1959 Surf Life Saving Championships, held at New Plymouth, were Peter Miller of Hamilton, Chas Lake of Wellington and Denis Quane of Christchurch. All three had been

(left) Joan Atherton at Ninety Mile Beach, Northland, 1961.

(inset) Joan showing off her second home-made board (sporting her initials), built by Bob around 1961.

PHOTOS BOB & JOAN ATHERTON

(below) The start of the paddle race at the 1959 national surf life saving champs at New Plymouth. Third from right is Rick Stoner with his polystyrene/fibreglass paddleboard built at the Piha Surf Life Saving Club. All the other competitors were using hollow longboards and Rick won the race by a significant margin. The appearance of the polystyrene boards at this meet led to several New Zealand surfers going back home to start building polystyrene Malibu boards.

PHOTO CHAS LAKE

(above, l to r) **Jim Mowtell and Chas Lake with a selection of early attempts at Malibu boards. Third from right is one of Peter Miller's hollow boards.**

concentrating on surfing longboards and trying to refine their designs to improve performance in the surf. In Rick and Bing's lightweight boards they suddenly saw a future which was full of new possibilities for surfing, but not necessarily surf life saving.

Also in attendance was Bart Smaill, from Dunedin. He had been concentrating on paddleboard racing but was getting proficient at standing up on the longboards and riding the waves. Bart recognised the future for board building when he experienced the comprehensive victory of the foam/fibreglass board in the paddleboard race.

The board builders returned to their respective homes of Auckland (Peter Byers), Hamilton (Peter Miller), Wellington (Chas Lake), Christchurch (Denis Quane) and Dunedin (Bart Smaill) to experiment with new board designs and materials, inspired by the Malibu boards of Rick Stoner and Bing Copeland. Surfing was on its way to a town near you.

At first, in Auckland ...

Sourcing the new materials and beginning to build the boards took some time. Peter Byers was at an advantage, having already toured Auckland with Rick and Bing to find the necessary components. As 1959 progressed, he began by glassing and finishing the shaped blanks that Rick and Bing had left behind. Peter's workshop was the glasshouse where he grew his tomatoes. He sold the boards to friends in the Piha Surf Life Saving Club who were eager to take up the new sport of surfing. He then set up a small surfboard factory in Valley Road, Piha.

Peter continued to use insulation polystyrene for a year and a half and built about 25-30 boards in that time. He used chopped strand fibreglass for two or three of the boards but fibreglass mat soon became available and, as it was much lighter than the chopped strand, it became the new standard. All the boards were sold to locals who wanted to take up surfing.

By 1961, Peter was attempting to blow his own foam blanks. He began by building a huge concrete mould, the top half of which he suspended from the ceiling, to be lowered onto its

other half once the foam ingredients had been added to the mould. At his first attempt, Peter was amazed to find that the expanding foam just lifted the big piece of concrete straight off again. He quickly refashioned the mould to have hinges on one side and clamps on the other. This proved able to contain the expanding foam but Peter does recall shearing half inch bolts clean off after having added too much foam on one occasion. (He never blew blanks in a fish pond, by the way. A movie once showed his mould lying open and filled with rainwater, and the comment was made that he should use the open mould as a goldfish pond. Legend has taken over from there.)

During these early days, Peter ran out of wood for fins so, needing something solid, he decided to try chopped strand fibreglass. It worked very well so he bought a roll of woven rovings (extra-heavy fibreglass mat) and started to make all his fins out of fibreglass. *'I was the first to do so, as far as I know, and when Bruce Brown visited New Zealand in 1961, he bought one to take back to California with him as he had never seen a fibreglass fin before.'*

Meanwhile, in Wellington...

Chas Lake had tried one of the Californian's Malibu boards at the 1959 national surf life saving champs and, although the surf was small, he found he could control his turns for the first time. He was amazed by the board's manoeuvrability and knew he had to have one. He convinced Bing to sell him the orange 10'6" paddleboard for £25 – a lot of money in 1959 (which he did not have with him) but he managed to borrow it from one of the surf life saving officials. Chas loaded the new board onto the Newmans bus and headed home to Wellington.

Chas arrived back in Wellington and immediately phoned his friend Jim 'Ace' Mowtel (also known as Mo). He was anxious to show Mo the new surfboard and demonstrate its attributes. *'Mo came round and picked me up in his "Ramset" wagon* [Mo worked for Ramset and had a company car] *and we headed for Houghton Bay, the only place in Wellington with a bit of a surf on the day. The waves were small and the wind onshore, and Mo was not convinced by his first viewing of the board in those messy conditions. The next day there were some clean waves at Lyall Bay and I was able to demonstrate the board properly. This time Mo was convinced.'*

They took the board to Mo's house and copied the shape of the board with a piece of chalk onto the concrete floor of his father's workshop, adding a couple of feet *'for more floatability'* and began work on the first fibreglass board made in Wellington.

They made the most of the contacts Mo had built up during his work with Ramset. At the building site for a meat company in Petone, coolstores were being constructed. Polystyrene blocks, which were used for insulating the coolstores, were coated with hot tar and stuck onto the concrete walls. Sometimes, the tar cooled too quickly and the polystyrene did not stick. These blocks were discarded. Mo salvaged them and, with a hand saw, cut off the side with the cold tar on. It left a polystyrene block about 8' long, 4' wide and 4-6" deep. Free foam!

A local company was making corrugated roofing from chopped strand fibreglass matting and from the roll of chopped strand there were always offcuts. Mo bought these offcuts cheaply and that took care of the fibreglass problem. The last thing needed was resin. *'A surf club friend worked for a resin manufacturer so we were able to purchase two gallon lots of resin at mates' rates. We were in business.'*

To protect the polystyrene from the ravages of the resin, they coated the foam blanks with Arolite glue and a liberal coating of Resene acrylic paint, also purchased at mates' rates. Decoration was applied (a few beer bottle labels, stripes made with electrician's tape, or travel poster cut outs of dusky maidens), resin was laid on and the result was a cheap but effective surfboard – the cost was just over £4.

And in Hamilton ...

Peter Miller returned to Hamilton after the 1959 champs, not with a genuine board but with all the information he could gather from Rick and Bing and plenty of enthusiasm for the new wave of surfboard construction. Peter says, *'Ace* [Jim Mowtel]

(above) Peter Miller showing great style while trying out one of his first polystyrene Malibu boards at Westshore Beach, Napier, 1959.

(right) Chas Lake with the Rick Stoner paddleboard he acquired *(right)* and the copy he and Jim Mowtell made *(left)*, named King Saud.

(below) An amazing collection of early New Zealand-made surfboards, displayed by some of our first surfers at Mount Maunganui, 1960. Note 'Gidg' made by Peter Miller, and the 'Made by Mo' surfboards built by Jim Mowtell.
(l to r) Richard Carr, Alf Lake (background), Peter Miller, Peter 'Ripper' Edwards, Jim 'Ace' Mowtel, Tony 'Bezel' Crosby, Peter Stevenson, Spencer Hemi (lying down).

(right) Denis Quane with his first Malibu board, built in his parents' backyard at Sumner, Christchurch, 1960.

(below) Bart Smaill riding at his favourite beach – Saint Clair, Dunedin, 1965.

PHOTO NEIL REID

PHOTO DENIS QUANE

Murray Bray *(left)* and Athol Murray *(below)* were amongst the first members of the Piha fraternity to take up surfing on the newly available boards, produced by Peter Byers. Piha, 1962.

PHOTO MURRAY BRAY

PHOTO ALAN GODFERY

and Chas immediately got into making foam and fibreglass boards, and so did I back in Hamilton. My first attempt wasn't very successful, however – it broke in half when I tried it out on Westshore Beach, Napier. What had happened was that the resin had eaten into the polystyrene foam I used to shape the board. A chance phone call to Ace and Chas put me right for the next board. I sealed the foam with Arolite glue before fibreglassing. Subsequently, I started splitting the boards down the middle and using thin redwood stringers and chopped strand fibreglass to strengthen the boards.'

While, in Christchurch ...

When Denis Quane saw the Malibu boards that Rick and Bing brought with them to New Plymouth, he was determined to go back to Christchurch and start building surfboards. He considered using balsa for his first boards but it was impossible to get hold of in Christchurch and too expensive to get anywhere else. However, Denis had started to read a bit about polystyrene boards that were being built in Australia, so he borrowed enough money to go to Sydney for a week where he stayed with distant relations in Manly.

He spent most days at the factory of Gordon Woods and Barry Bennett learning as much as he could about building foam boards. He returned to New Zealand with some blanks but couldn't import any more because of the restrictions on import licences.

By the beginning of the 1960s, Denis was still running up against obstacles to building Malibu boards and it became apparent that he had to find a way of making his own blanks.

And finally, in Dunedin ...

Bart Smaill arrived back in Dunedin armed with instructions from Rick and Bing on how to build a Malibu board. He went straight to the local hardware shop for materials – insulation foam, fibreglass mat and resin. The instructions weren't quite comprehensive enough, however, and Bart's first attempt resulted in the resin dissolving the foam. A switch to epoxy resin rectified that problem and his first Malibu board was soon in the water.

Bart built his boards primarily for paddleboard racing but the lighter Malibu boards were much more manoeuvrable than the old longboards so surfing them became easier. Soon the surfing qualities of the boards became the focus and Bart was producing two types of board for himself and members of the Saint Clair Surf Life Saving Club – the surfboard and the paddleboard.

Most of the recipients of the new boards continued to ride waves lying down or kneeling but, over the next two to three years, a few took up the new art of surfing – Graeme Nesbitt, Eddie Moretty, Gary Jacobson and Trevor Clark.

The swell picks up

It is interesting to stand at Piha on a busy summer day and look out at the hordes of surfers and swimmers, and imagine Peter Byers, Peter Way and Murray Bray, and a few others of the surf club, as the only surfers on the bar in those early days of 1959-60.

Murray Bray: *'There were only about four local riders to begin with at Piha – Peter Byers, Buddy Cox, Roger Curtis and myself. I still have a board built by Peter Byers from those first days after Rick and Bing left. The first board riding competition I can remember was at Piha in about 1961 between local surf life savers who were keen on surfing. The competition included some visitors from Muriwai. For me, surfing was mainly restricted to beaches with surf life saving facilities as I was still successfully competing in surf life saving competitions and would take my surfboard to the meetings. The clubs also offered a place to stay if the surf was good. There were so few of us surfing initially that we never had to chase surf for seclusion and, in fact, the company of other surfers was a pleasant novelty.'*

The 1960s meant a lot of different things to different people but for surfing it was a period of huge growth. It took a few years to get the industry up to speed but, by the middle of the decade, surfing was growing faster than any other sport in history. For example, in 1960, there were perhaps half a dozen board builders in the country and about 50-100 surfers. By 1963, it is estimated that there were approximately 300 surfers in the entire country and about 10 board builders. By 1966-67, the main

board builders would be each producing about 40 boards per week over summer, a total of 3500 a year, supplying an estimated 15,000 surfers.

Also, there were no official surfing competitions in 1960. The first national surfing championships were held in 1963 at Mount Maunganui, after which the New Zealand Surf Riders' Association was formed. By 1969, national teams had already been travelling overseas for three years, there were around 30 local board riders clubs, there was an interclub trophy (the Quane Trophy) and there was simmering discontent over competitive surfing.

New Zealand's first alternative culture?

Peter Fitzsimmons started surfing in Wellington in 1959-60 on a Chas Lake/Jim Mowtell board. *'As the 60s progressed and society went through some significant growing pains, surfing probably represented the first true 'alternative culture' in New Zealand. Surfing had a true 'soul' to it which was missing from the rest of the country. It involved total commitment and an intimate connection*

PHOTO BOB COMER

(above) **Campbell Ross was one of the top surfers in the country in the early 60s:** *'Surfing was an intense freedom and the lifestyle took us out of deadening suburbs and conservative expectations.'*

PHOTO MIKE GARDINER

(left) **When there was no surf, garden bars were a favourite place to spend time and swap surf stories.** *(l to r)* **Quentin Simpson, Unknown, Blake Morse (hat), Keith Wakely (rear), Mike Gardiner, Rex Banks, Wayne Blundell, Dave Littlejohn during their epic '9' session (everyone drank nine bottles of beer), New Plymouth, 1961. The '9' session resulted in Rex Banks 'surfing' the car bonnet past the nurses' quarters in town, losing his balance and ending up in the hospital with serious grazing.**

PHOTO CHAS LAKE

(right, l to r) **Chas Lake and Jim Mowtell demonstrating that any car would do once the boards were light enough. This photo was taken outside the Maranui Surf Life Saving Club in Wellington, 1960.**

PHOTO PETER MILLER

(above) **Peter Miller (centre) and friends playing up on the beach at Mount Maunganui, 1961. Surfers' behaviour tended to make them stand out wherever they went.**

with the water. It moved away from team-based sport and it was an opportunity for young people to experiment with lifestyle.'

Quite quickly, a significant number of young people were reorganising their lives to accommodate their new passion for surfing. They began to drop out of organised sports groups (surf life saving being the most obvious example), and abandoned established social groups and even jobs because of surfing. They discovered a new freedom in the waves, new friends, new skills and an alternative lifestyle that was healthy and invigorating.

Campbell Ross: *'Surfing was an intense freedom and the lifestyle took us out of deadening suburbs and conservative expectations. I had been "expected" to go into accountancy of all things. I think I flipped most firmly into surfing when I looked up from columns of figures at a plastered concrete wall one hot and muggy January morning in Hamilton and knew life really was a beach, somewhere out there.'*

The sport did follow other social trends of the 60s, towards drug experimentation, loads of drinking and getting away from the 'establishment'. Surf parties were legendary and frequently attracted party crashers from outside the surf culture, for example, showdowns with the 'Rockers'. 'A bit of biff' at the parties was a frequent occurrence and added to the somewhat tarnished image that the general public was developing about surfers.

There were still very few surfers in the early 60s and that

made them a special group – and they revelled in the exclusivity. Visiting surfers from overseas gave hints and samples of what surfers in their home towns were wearing, and the locals soon started dressing differently from mainstream New Zealand. A number of local surfers started travelling overseas and would return home with the latest in surf music, clothing and magazines. (Overseas travel was still a relatively uncommon pursuit for young New Zealanders in the early 60s and surfers may have been the precursors of the OE [overseas experience] generations of the future.)

In a relatively short period of time, there was a new social/ sporting group in New Zealand who were exercising differently, acting differently, dressing differently, listening to different music, who drank and partied copiously, and who drove all over the country in big cars to pursue a sport that few understood. New Zealand society was still conservative by nature and the idea of a whole group developing outside the established boundaries led to suspicion. Surfers were quickly deemed to be somewhat undesirable.

They were, however, still a small group and there was an important revolution to occur in 1960 before surfing as a sport really took off. And it all had to do with weight.

Who rules the beaches?

As a new breed of surfers began to appear on the beaches in 1960, supplied with boards by the fledgling surfboard industry, the first challenge to surf life saving's dominance of the beach occurred.

Surf life savers stored their longboards at their club because they were immensely heavy – no one wanted to carry a 70-pound board to and from home. However, with a new foam and fibreglass Malibu board, that weighed about 30 pounds, you could carry it without too much trouble and, best of all, you could put it on top of a car and take it wherever you wanted to.

During the 1950s, people were starting to earn more money and the price of cars was decreasing. Consequently, private cars became more and more common in New Zealand. By the early 60s, many people could get to the beaches in their own car, and if they had bought a new Malibu board, they could take that to the beach on the car. And then they could take it home again, or to another beach, without having to leave it at the local surf life saving club because of its weight.

All of a sudden, the surf life saving club was not the centre of all surf activity at the beach and, what's more, the clubs had no control over this new sport of surfing. Lightweight boards and the car had created a new species on the beach – the surfer. A surfer could now function independently of surf life saving and go to any beach they chose. But why go to other beaches?

Surfing on longboards had involved very little manoeuvrability on waves and mainly riding straight into the beach. With the new Malibu boards, it was easy, and desirable if you wanted a better ride, to surf along the face of the waves. This meant that the shape of the waves was important to surfing because a better face on the wave meant a longer and faster ride. Thus, tide, wind and beach shape all conspired to give different quality waves.

These aspects of modern surfing resulted in surfers discovering that their local beach would produce certain types of waves, good or bad, and that other types of waves could be found by travelling to other beaches. The travel had to coincide with the correct wind and tide conditions in order to make it worth the trip and the expense. So, a surfer had to be able to go when natural conditions dictated and not be harnessed by other commitments, such as surf life saving patrols (and jobs in extreme cases).

As the commitment to surfing increased, commitment to other responsibilities decreased. This didn't mean that all surfers gave up surf life saving because, frequently, their local beach had good surf and they could maintain both interests anyway. There was also still a strong sense of commitment to the friends and duties of the surf life saving club.

Of those first surfers in New Zealand who already had a strong bond with surf life saving, almost all maintained that relationship and fitted their surfing into it, a little bit at the expense of surf life

PHOTO BOB COMER

(left) Shelter built by The Point locals at Raglan Beach for protection from the winter elements, 1963.

(below, l to r) Quentin Simpson, Blake Morse, Richard Gardiner, Keith Wakely and Wayne Blundell with early boards and surfwagon at Piha, 1960. The advent of 'lightweight' polystyrene Malibu boards meant that surfers could load up a car and go anywhere they wanted to without being tied to a surf life saving club.

PHOTO MIKE GARDINER

PHOTO PETER BYERS COLLECTION

(above) **Most of the early visiting surfers came from the USA. This picture shows** *(l to r)* **Bruce Browne, Sam Deikelman, Peter Byers and John Paine at Piha, 1961.**
In 1960, Bruce Brown was touring the Pacific and filming *Surfing Hollow Days.* **He called into New Zealand, did a bit of filming and checked some locations for his next movie. With him was Phil Edwards. They both stayed at Tim Murdoch's house where another Californian surfer, Sam Deikelman, was already in residence. Says Tim:** *'Sam used to sleep on the floor, much to my mother's surprise, and liked to stare out to sea for long periods of time – he was a true surf hippie. His father was a big-wig in the US Airforce. One day we received a visit from the local US ambassador to inform Sam that if he did not go home immediately, he would be arrested when he eventually did return to the US. He decided to return home that week.'*
During a trip to Piha, Tim introduced the visitors to Peter Byers. Peter remembers Phil Edwards as one of the most impressive surfers he has seen. Phil had a balsa board with him with which he really impressed the local surfers. Some footage of his surfing at Piha can be seen in *Surfing Hollow Days,* **as can a nose ride by Sam Deikelman.**

(below) **An advertisement for Frank Wilkin's** *Kahuna* **surfboards from the back page of New Zealand's first surf magazine,** *New Zealand Surfer* **.**

saving perhaps. But the new, young surfers (gremmies/grommets) who came into the sport after 1960, with no background in surf life saving, seldom took up the noble beach service, preferring instead to dedicate all their spare time to surfing.

New recruits

As more families visited the beach and saw surfers for the first time, new young recruits started requesting their own boards from the early board builders. Unlike the first few who got involved in the sport of surfing, there was now some information available on how to be a surfer. Boards, some magazines and even early movies were becoming available. There were other surfers around to learn from (including the social behaviour associated with the sport) and good breaks were being discovered all the time. The infrastructure for a surfing lifestyle was falling into place.

As more people arrived at the beach and wanted to take up surfing, the demand for boards increased. Many tried making their own boards, due to their scarcity and the high cost of a new board (up to £40), but soon discovered that the materials and skills for making a quality surfboard were not easily acquired.

A second group of surfers began producing boards in the early 60s, to fill the needs of the increasing surfing population. They sprang up all over the country but most frequently in Auckland where the sport got off to an early start and where there was a greater number of potential surfers.

An industry is born

By 1960, Peter Byers had established himself as *the* board supplier to the Piha surfing community and was probably the only commercial producer of surfboards in the country. Others such as Ace Mowtell and Chas Lake, Denis Quane and Peter Miller were getting close to commercial production. However, Peter's work with Rick and Bing, and his knowledge of where to get supplies, had allowed him to get a head start in the fledgling surfboard industry.

continued on page 27

Peter Byers

Peter was one of the very first in New Zealand to surf and build Malibu boards. He was definitely the first to manufacture surfboards on a commercial basis, and his pioneering work laid the foundation for a whole generation of board builders in Auckland and beyond.

Peter lived at Piha beach, in Auckland, and of all the surf life savers who saw Rick Stoner and Bing Copeland surfing their Malibu boards for the first time at Piha, Peter was the one who really pursued the new sport of surfing. When Peter saw how they surfed across the face of the waves and the ease with which they manoeuvred their boards, he was smitten by the surf bug. He surfed as much as possible and worked alongside them when they built two polystyrene paddleboards in the Piha Surf Life Saving Club.

Peter epitomises the spirit of the early surfers, showing dedication and determination to pursue the sport of surfing when it was only in its infancy, and yet maintaining his involvement in, and commitment to, surf life saving. As the years went by, and surfing became more popular, it was a tricky balancing act due to the acrimony between surfers and surf life savers and the continuing defections to surfing from the ranks of surf life saving. By the simple act of giving his best to both sports Peter avoided having to take sides.

His determination to be a board builder was displayed by his ability to create an industry where there was none. Peter scoured Auckland for the necessary materials to support his new business of board building, and as the demand for boards grew throughout the 60s, he supplied blanks to other board makers such as Bob Davie, Peter Way, Dave Jackman and many others.

Experimenting with custom shapes for Peter Byers Surfboards was Peter's true passion. His shaping was influenced by the boards of Reynolds Yater which came to New Zealand with visiting surfers. Magazines and movies from the USA, when available, also offered some inspiration but Peter shaped using his own sense of what made a board perform well, and plenty of R & D in the water. He made all his own boards but never got to keep them for long as someone would invariably make him an offer soon after he took them out into the waves.

Peter was offered the opportunity to go to California and do some shaping in Phil Edwards' factory but he decided to get married and stay on at Piha with his new wife Margaret. Peter describes Phil Edwards as one of the best surfers he has ever seen after he got to spend some time with him in the waves at Piha. *'He is one of those people who waves just seem to come to them.'*

Peter has never gone off on international surf trips, being content with his idyllic lifestyle at Piha. He has four children, all of whom surf. He no longer surfs himself, finding it too crowded, and now prefers to go fishing.

(below) **Peter surfing his favourite spot – the Piha Bar, 1962, and not another soul in sight.**

PHOTO ALAN GODFERY

(right) Peter Byers surfing the Piha Bar, Auckland 1960. The photo was taken by John Severson and published as a double-page spread in *The Saturday Evening Post* in the USA.

PHOTO JOHN SEVERSON

CUSTOM BUILT
SURFBOARDS
BY
Peter Byers
PIHA

I sat with Peter on the balcony of his new house, overlooking the surf at Piha, and while he reminisced about those first days of surfing with himself and maybe one or two others out, we watched the usual dozens (sometimes hundreds) of surfers battle for waves at South Piha. Peter still looks strong and fit, and I could imagine him just stepping back into a shaping room. However, he is now content to enjoy the satisfying, surfing-free lifestyle at Piha that I think he thoroughly deserves.

More surf club members were getting interested in surfing and there were steady orders for Peter. As interest picked up and he found it difficult to meet demand, new board builders began to step into the market. Almost all of them started by coming to Peter for advice and to purchase blanks. Peter was the main supplier of blanks to Auckland board builders throughout the early 60s, and he also supplied a number of other centres throughout New Zealand.

One of the first new entrants to the Auckland surfboard market was Frank Wilkin. Frank was a beach lover who was involved to a small degree with the Bethells and Piha Surf Life Saving Clubs. He did enough patrols to be able to stay at the beach but quickly gave up surf life saving when surfing 'arrived' at Piha with Rick and Bing. Frank started surfing in the summer of 1959-60 after seeing Rick, Bing and Peter Byers at Piha.

A steady flow of American visitors (such as Phil Edwards, John Severson, Fred van Dyke, Bruce Browne and others) in the early 60s brought better and better boards which local production could not match at that point. Frank was already working in a company that produced fibreglass display models, and it was an easy transition to start making fibreglass surfboards. After getting advice and a blank from Peter Byers, Frank built his first board in the basement of his parents' house in 1961.

Frank soon built his own moulds and started producing pop-out boards from his parents' basement. The original moulds, for a 9'4" and a 9'6" production board, served Frank well for many years. He produced pop-outs, under the name Kahuna, and also custom boards under the name Frank Wilkin Surfboards.

The pop-outs were quick to produce, had a guaranteed shape, and could help meet the soaring demand for boards from new surfers. As surfers improved their skills and awareness of how boards performed, they would start ordering custom boards that met their unique requirements.

Like Denis Quane, Frank got his first foam from Maurice Cosgrove in Takapuna, and again like Denis, he soon found it to be inappropriate for custom surfboards. AC Hatrix Limited

PHOTO ALAN GODFERY

(left, l to r) **John Paine, Tim Murdoch, Unknown, Unknown at Piha, Auckland, 1961.**

came to the rescue, importing the ingredients for polyurethane foam. So while Frank experimented to his heart's content with the custom boards, he kept the burgeoning surfboard market fed with the Kahuna pop-outs.

Another person to arrive on the surf scene at the beginning of the 1960s was Tim Murdoch. Tim brought a different dimension to the early surf environment with his enthusiasm for photography, travel and an entrepreneurial approach to the sport.

Tim started surfing in the 1950s on a hollow ply board that was used by many of the locals at Langs Beach. He moved, with his family, to Auckland in the mid 1950s but still spent each summer at Langs Beach. He was involved to a minor degree in surf life saving but only did enough duty to be able to stay at the clubrooms at the beach. He quickly separated from the surf life saving movement when Malibu surfing arrived in New Zealand.

Tim first saw Malibu boards during a trip to Hawaii in 1959 and even tried out surfing on these new boards. He didn't have enough money to bring a board back to New Zealand but, by then, Rick and Bing had introduced the Malibu board to Piha.

Tim and his good friend, John Paine, met up with 'Bogginga' Bob Ryan, who lived in Otahuhu, and he took them for a trip out to Piha on the back of his Chevy truck. There they met Peter

PHOTO ALAN GODFERY

PHOTO ALAN GODFERY

Tim Murdoch *(top)* **and John Paine** *(bottom)* **surfing Piha during those first uncrowded years, 1960-62.**

(above) **Denis Quane's very rustic backyard surfboard operation in Sumner, Christchurch, 1962. In the foreground is one of the first moulds he built.**

(right) **Jim Mowtell's 'Ramset' station wagon at Raglan, April 1963. The trailer was a converted bomb carrier and was used to transport 'Made by Mo' boards. He would sell the boards wherever a surf trip took him.**

Byers and first experienced the modern, light surfboards that Peter was building. With these new lighter boards, Tim became totally hooked on surfing. *'We just went nuts on surfing. We would drive all over the country looking for waves. We would spend weekends in the Coromandel where we would behave really badly and surf as much as we could. It was great!'*

John Paine was a school friend of Tim Murdoch. John fell in love with surfing after that trip to Piha. He and Tim immediately started making their own boards after getting blanks and advice from Peter Byers. They produced enough to supply their friends but soon gave away making their own boards when the bigger producers, such as Atlas Woods, Quane and Dunlop, got going in the early 1960s.

South of the Bombay Hills ...

Prior to 1963, the industry outside Auckland was restricted mainly to the same starters from the late-1950s, Denis Quane, Peter Miller and Jim Mowtell.

Denis Quane went to Auckland to try and buy the chemicals for making foam blanks from Maurice Cosgrove who was based in an old house in Takapuna. Maurice supplied the necessary chemicals and also gave Denis some ideas on how to build a mould for blowing the foam – make the shape out of fibreglass and reinforce it with copper pipes. Denis built the mould in his

backyard as soon as he got back to Christchurch.

By now, his father was helping him and their first attempts to blow the foam ended up with them blowing the mould to bits, so it was back to the drawing board.

Denis constructed a new steel mould, with clamps, and made his first 9'6" production board. The mould was lined with chopped mat and then the foam was poured in and the steel lids closed and clamped shut. It was produced in two halves which were joined together with a half-inch wooden stringer, lightly sanded and glassed with a layer of 10-ounce resin. Finally, a ply laminated fin was glassed onto the back.

The blanks were all done in Sumner, in Denis' backyard, and the rest of the production took place in the back of a shop he had leased in Sumner township in 1962. Denis used the foam supplied by Maurice Cosgrove for a couple of years but it was refrigeration foam and, while adequate for pop-outs, it was not appropriate for custom boards. He kept pleading with the Trade and Industry Department in Wellington to give him an import licence to bring in the chemicals for real polyurethane foam for making custom boards. This was at a time when import licences were required for anything you wanted to bring into New Zealand and the licences were very hard to get. It was 1965 before he was finally granted an import licence.

In Wellington, Chas Lake left the surfboard production to Jim Mowtell soon after the construction of their first few boards, and concentrated on surfing. He and Mo would travel up and down the east and west coasts from Wellington, surfing previously undiscovered surf spots and seeing very few other surfers. *'If we ever saw another car with surfboards, we knew who it was; there were very few surfers around in those early years.'*

They began to travel to Taranaki, Raglan, Mahia and Gisborne. They were so enthusiastic that they would surf right through winter, without wetsuits, using old football jerseys and cut off woollen trousers to keep warm. Mo would hook up an old trailer to his Ramset wagon and load it with the boards he had made, and sell them to interested surfers during their travels.

Consequently, 'Made by Mo' boards appeared at many beaches outside the Wellington area.

In Hamilton, Peter Miller was getting up to speed on board building after his initial failure in Napier. *'Those first lightweight boards were very popular and before long I was building them for surfers at the Mount, Whakatane and as far away as Gisborne. Many an hour was spent at the Mount Surf Club discussing rail shapes.*

'Unfortunately, early surf riders wanted more and more extras on their boards such as three and four stringers, tail blocks and even double glassing to stop dings. All this added to the weight and loss of performance. These boards were great for big-wave riding at Raglan but not for the smaller east coast surf.

'The foam boards that we built in 1959-61 were a good start but, in 1962, shorter and lighter boards started coming out of California and performing on waves like nothing we had seen before. The whole beach scene was taking off with young teenagers wanting to take up surfing. Copies of Surfing World *were starting to filter into the country and resulted in customers rushing in wanting copies of boards they had seen in the magazine. The orders were stacking up and I got Peter Byers to supply me with foam blanks.*

'Even boardshorts came in. I can still see Bob Comer (a red head) wearing bright red and purple shorts down past his knees. My sister Marilyn went to America in 1960-61 and brought back the designs for the shorter Californian surfboards which, because of their shape, we called "pig" boards.

'Marilyn was one of the first Malibu riders in New Zealand, as far as I know. She started on a shorter and lighter version of the boards and rode at the Mount and in Wellington. Chas Lake and Mo called her "Gidget" after the character in the movie.

'Discussions I have had recently with Gordon Woods, in Australia, indicate that during the early 60s, New Zealand was right up with them in terms of design and materials used, once we had got over the lag period of the 1950s.'

Peter continued to build boards for the burgeoning surf market and, in 1962, opened the Inland Surf Shop in Hamilton.

Campbell Ross also lived in Hamilton and saw the boards

PHOTO PETER MILLER

PHOTO RICK BRADLEY

(left) Peter Miller (far left) surfing The Point at Raglan, 1962. Peter is thought to have been the first to surf The Point, on a longboard, in 1959.

(left below) Campbell Ross was one of the country's best surfers in the early 60s and one of the first to surf The Point, Raglan. Bob Comer: *'I heard rumours about how good Campbell was when I started surfing in 1962. He was in Australia then but when he got back I quickly saw that the rumours were true.'*

(below) Jim Mowtel at Raglan, 1961. The car is a classic example of the early surfwagon that helped liberate surfers and set them exploring the coastline of New Zealand.

PHOTO CHAS LAKE

(right) **Waipu Cove, Northland, October 1963. An exotic shelter built by the Whangarei surfers while the surf was flat.** (l to r) Rod Finlayson, Kit Steer and Tui Wordley.

(below) **Rod 'Prod' Finlayson at Waipu Cove, October 1963.**

PHOTO TUI WORDLEY

PHOTO TUI WORDLEY

PHOTO TUI WORDLEY

(right, l to r) **Rex Whitelaw, Max Leonard, Unknown, Max McGregor, Unknown, Tui Wordley and David Woodman, Waipu Cove, February 1962. The photo shows a great selection of the first locally made boards. The shapes are very different from those that appeared elsewhere in the country, and look remarkably like boards from a later era.**

Peter Miller was producing. Campbell started surfing in 1960 on a board he had built himself. Over the next two to three years he went on to build about 30 boards, for himself and for sale. Most were in the 9'6" to 10' range but he experimented down to 6'.

Campbell was one of the first to surf Raglan and dominated there as a goofy footer. He also spent plenty of time over at Mount Maunganui when conditions suited. *'1960-61 was a major transitional period for surfing at Mount Maunganui where I began to surf. There were still hollow longboards being ridden but there was also a colourful fleet of home-made fibreglass boards, experimental in shape, quite long and highly decorated.*

'The thing about both of these early groups, on wood and on the first fibreglass, was that they rode in pretty much fixed positions. The big revolution came when a few of us began to move around on our boards – mobility and weight transfer were the keys to Malibu riding. I remember when Ace Mowtel and I caught a wave together at the Mount – I rode literally around him, underneath and back over the top – that was the difference in manoeuvrability if you walked.'

One of the more remarkable early surfboard builders was Jim McCulloch of Gisborne. Jim owned a company that built fibreglass boats which went by the name of Condor Craft. Around 1962, Jim saw some pictures of Hawaiians with fibreglass Malibus and decided to try and build one for his son Keith. The Condor Craft surfboards were about 8'6" long and made of two moulded fibreglass halves (a deck and a bottom) that were stuck together once a shaped core of insulation foam had been added. The join would come apart if there was any rough treatment and the boards leaked. Sand was added to the deck for traction but when that was found to be too rough, a serrated aluminium plate was put into the mould to give the fibreglass deck a texture.

Keith McCulloch: *'The boards served a purpose in the absence of true Malibu boards but they were short lived because real Malibus and Bob Davie soon came to town. They were OK for kids but not for serious surfers.'* About 20-30 Condor Craft surfboards were made with a few still surviving today in Gisborne.

And the rest made do

Many of the new surfers began by building their own boards, partly because of the difficulty of buying a board and partly because of the expense of new boards. This was particularly true in areas outside of Auckland, Christchurch, Hamilton and Wellington where our pioneers were at work.

In Northland, Bob and Joan Atherton were still surfing in isolation and building their own boards. There were no surfboards, magazines or visitors to give them an indication of what was happening in the outside world of surfing.

A little further to the south, in Whangarei, Tui Wordley was discovering surfing in 1961. *'I originally became interested in surfing after seeing some very early magazine pictures and newsreels at the movies. In the early summer of 1961, I was at Langs Beach and I saw a group of people sitting on the beach, among whom were Tim Murdoch and John Paine, and they had two Malibu boards with them. I had a close look at the boards, and decided then and there that I had to make one for myself.*

'My first board was home made using polystyrene foam blanks measuring 6' x 3' x 4" which were used for insulation in the building trade. The offcuts from the corners were glued to the ends to give extra length, resulting in a finished board measuring around 8'6". We used three-ply wood stringers and a heavy plywood for a fat, double-edged fin. After shaping (hacking?), the whole lot was sealed and glassed. Design ideas came from magazines and from people who had been overseas, and others came purely from our imagination.

'The first time I stood up on a surfboard was in June/July of 1961, at Waipu Cove, in a small shore break. Myself and the Edge brothers, Ross and Don, tried out our three different boards. After we had been surfing for about a year, the clubbies at Waipu and Ruakaka started making themselves boards.

'In the first two years we mostly surfed Waipu Cove, Langs Beach, Sandy Bay, Pataua, Ruakaka and Mangawhai Heads. Many of the spots we surfed were possibly surfed for the first time ever, although we were not certain. Later we travelled farther

PHOTO TUI WORDLEY

(above, l to r) Ross Edge and Tui Wordley. Tui: *'The first time I stood up on a surfboard was in June/July of 1961, at Waipu Cove, in a small shore break. Myself and the Edge brothers, Ross and Don, tried out our three different boards. Ross's mum took this photo with my Box Brownie camera.'*

(left, l to r) Rod Finlayson, Kit Steer and Tui Wordley, Oakura camping ground, Taranaki, 1963: *'The pot contains rabbit stew given to us by the campers in the next site. We met the* Endless Summer *boys at Raglan on this trip – they had just come from trout fishing at Rotorua.'*

PHOTO TUI WORDLEY

(left) On the old Ruakaka to Waipu road, Northland, 1962. *(l to r)* 'Gibbo' Gibson, Chris Frazerhurst, Rex Whiteman, Norm Baker and Tui Wordley.

(above) **Taranaki pioneers Wayne Arthur *(top)*, Gerald Turner *(middle)* and Billy Walsh *(bottom)* showing their style at Waiwhakaiho, New Plymouth, 1962.**

afield to Ahipara (Shipwreck Bay), Ocean Beach, Piha, Paradise Bay, Mimi Whangata (The Farm), Baileys, Raglan, New Plymouth, Gisborne, Mount Maunganui and Whangamata.

'At one stage, we built a concrete mould with chicken wire reinforcement and steel band clamps but after three or four failed attempts the mould finally cracked and we realised that it was too hard to work out the correct mixtures for the foam. Also, the influx of Yank and Australian surfers meant we could buy boards from surfers who were returning home.'

For the new surf recruits in Taranaki, there was again an absence of information that would give an indication of what was happening in the outside world of surfing. Peter Quinn, Leith Beaurepaire and Dave Littlejohn were joined in the surf by a few dozen new surfers, including Billy Walsh, Wayne Arthur and Gerald Turner, and a good number of women surfers including Trish Dwyer, Diane Saywell, Lyn Humphreys, Suzie Curzons and Marge Harvey. Most were riding home-made boards from the backyards of surfers such as Gig Bailey. Wayne Arthur: *'I started surfing around 1962 after seeing the first bunch of New Plymouth surfers at Mikotahi. I was mesmerised by their abilities but as a skinny Health Camp reject, there was no way I felt brave enough to ask for a turn. With an advance on next year's*

(below) **Ken Griffin with his home-made 9'8" Malibu board, Napier, 1961. Proudly displayed in front of the cars of the day – (l to r) Vauxhall Victor, Ford 315 and Fiat Bambina.**

pocket money, my mate Ray Rowson and I built our own board. My money and his enthusiasm and craft skills meant it was a joint venture but the thing was an absolute disaster. The resin ate through the sealer and dissolved about two thirds of the board. Luckily, we hadn't thrown away the offcuts and shavings, so we made up a slurry and poured it into the pitted remains. Somehow we finished it and took it to Back Beach to launch the mighty beast – it was about 8' long and 2' wide. After the third wave, it broke in two along with my dreams and resolve. I cannot remember ever being so devastated. We were both 13 and young enough to cry. The next week, my sister, bless her heart, loaned me 25 quid to buy a repaired Peter Way from Dave Littlejohn.'

Dave Littlejohn had opened the New Plymouth Surf Shop in 1962 which initially stocked Quane and Dunlop boards. The local surfers suddenly had a good supply of the latest equipment available and backyard building quickly diminished.

Ken Griffin was the local barber in Napier and a member of the surf life saving club. He remembers Malibu surfboard riding starting in Napier in 1961 after two Napier Surf Life Saving Club members called into Hawaii on the way home from the United Kingdom. They were amazed to see the Hawaiian surfers riding short, lightweight boards made from foam and fibreglass (at that time, the only thing resembling a surfboard at the Napier Surf Life Saving Club were two 16-foot hollow plywood boards, each weighing approximately 60 pounds).

In the middle of 1961, the first successful foam and fibreglass Malibu boards were made in Napier by Ken Griffin, Bob Crozier, Barry Jones and John Baker. The boards were made from shaped insulation foam which was sealed with Arolite glue, then covered with chopped strand fibreglass mat and resin. They learnt the hard way about using glue to protect the foam from the resin, even after seeing Peter Miller snap his first board at Westshore because of the weakened foam.

Ken Griffin: *'The only plans we had were 9'6" long, 4" deep, 22" wide, rounded on the rails and both ends, and finished with a 10" fin on the bottom. The boards actually turned out well – very buoyant, and easy to paddle and stand on. We went on to make about 15 boards for the local surfers over the next couple of years.*

'However, these were not the first foam and fibreglass boards to be made in Napier. A year earlier, Noel Tolhurst and Noel Hatton had attempted to make two boards from the new materials but the fibreglass came away from the foam and the shapes were flat and square compared with the rounded Malibu shape.

'We started riding at Westshore, coming straight in on the waves like bodysurfing, but after visits from Peter Miller, Jim Mowtell and Ray Trilford, we started cutting across the waves.'

All around the country, new surfers were making their own boards in order to get into the waves. Surfers, in general, were still few and far between but the numbers were increasing as they were fed new boards from the fledgling industry and enthusiasts' backyards. Sufficient boards were being produced to satisfy local areas, and the early manufacturers were starting to send boards around the country to the first surf shops that were opening (often as part of another business, for example, Dave Littlejohn's surf shop was at the front of his existing canvas/saddlery shop, and Ken Griffin sold boards from a corner of his barber shop). Surfers in more remote locations could become 'beach agents' for one of the board builders and supply any local enthusiasts.

The market was increasing quickly as the 60s progressed and demand generally outstripped production. Backyard board building soon decreased as a second-hand board market began to emerge and the quality of the new boards improved to a point that made home-built boards an unattractive option.

Just surfing

Not everyone tried to make their own boards. Throughout the country, there was a growing number of individuals who just bought a board and went surfing.

In Auckland, people such as Peter Way, Mike Gardiner, Murray Bray, Buddy Cox and Roger Curtis were purchasing boards from Peter Byers and spending as much time as possible

PHOTO MIKE GARDINER

(above) Mike Gardiner (left), Quentin Simpson (back) and Peter Russell-Green (front) at Pakiri Beach, Northland, 1960. The beach fire is one of the lasting images of dedicated surfing in the early 60s. There were no wetsuits so the fire was the best way to warm up enough before going out to catch some more waves.

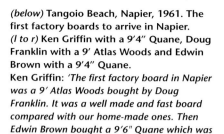

(below) Tangoio Beach, Napier, 1961. The first factory boards to arrive in Napier. (l to r) Ken Griffin with a 9'4" Quane, Doug Franklin with a 9' Atlas Woods and Edwin Brown with a 9'4" Quane.
Ken Griffin: *'The first factory board in Napier was a 9' Atlas Woods bought by Doug Franklin. It was a well made and fast board compared with our home-made ones. Then Edwin Brown bought a 9'6" Quane which was very light and easy to turn.'*

PHOTO KEN GRIFFIN

PHOTO MIKE GARDINER

(left) Mike Gardiner surfing the Piha Bar, May, 1962. This is probably one of the first water shots of surfing taken in New Zealand.

PHOTO RICK BRADLEY

(left) Bob Comer, Point Board Riders pioneer. 'Surfing was great for me because it was an individual pursuit, I got to see a lot of the country and I was able to indulge my passion for photography. I was seen as a bit of an enforcer but I never picked a fight. However, I was prepared to stand up to trouble makers.'

(right, l to r) Paul Griffin, Tim Murdoch, Ray Cates and Tony Griffin attending the 1964 nationals at Mount Maunganui. The Griffin brothers were in the forefront of surfing in Wellington, while Tim and Ray were well known Auckland pioneers.

PHOTO GEOFF LOGAN, PHOTO NEWS

(right) Gisborne's surfing pioneers. (l to r) John Logan, Peter Goodwin, Darryl Heighway, Dave Swan and Kevin Pritchard. John Logan: 'We were preparing to venture out over the rocks at Makarori, about 1962. The car is my little 105E Ford Anglia which worked pretty hard in those days transporting five young men and their 10' boards. I'm wearing typical pre-wetsuit gear of the day – a pair of shorts and a woolly jersey.'

PHOTO JOHN LOGAN

in the surf at Piha. On the North Shore of Auckland, surfers were beginning to appear at Takapuna Beach on home-made boards and boards brought back from Australia and the USA.

There were very few surfers in Wellington in the early 1960s and all were known to each other. Most trips involved the same few surfers – Chas Lake, Jim Mowtell, Paddy Perkinson, Peter Fitzsimmons, Paul Griffin and Tony Griffin – and every trip out of Wellington involved the discovery of new and unsurfed locations. They frequently travelled to Gisborne and Mahia for the weekend, or up the west coast to New Plymouth and Raglan. All of today's popular spots were empty and previously unridden when these surfers arrived in the early 1960s.

Larry Foster began surfing in 1960, as a 7-year-old, at Otaki Beach, north of Wellington. Larry belonged to the Otaki Surf Life Saving Club but was seduced into a life of surfing. 'My first surf trip was with my mates from Otaki, in an old van, 20 miles down the coast to Paekakariki. I remember seeing Ride The Wild Surf, starring Fabian, and thought it was so cool – I was hooked after that.'

In Hamilton, Bob Comer, Rick Bradley, Robin Hood and an increasing number of other surfers were sourcing surfboards from Peter Miller and driving out to Raglan to surf The Point, or travelling to Whangamata and The Mount for east coast surf.

Gisborne pioneer surfers, John Logan and Kevin Pritchard, remember seeing their first Malibu boards at a surf life saving carnival in Gisborne around 1959. Over the next year, Malibu boards started to filter into Gisborne via visitors to the area from Hamilton and Wellington. John and Kevin, together with other surf life savers turned surfers Dave Swan, Peter Goodwin and Darryl Heighway, became the nucleus of local surfers. These five were amongst the first to surf Makarori Point. John remembers it taking them a few weeks of watching the point before they plucked up the courage to surf the break because they were wary of the rocks, especially in those pre-legrope days.

Dave Swan: 'I belonged to Midway Surf Life Saving Club. The club had a longboard which I surfed on until I got a surfboard in

1961. *Soon after that first board, I got a Peter Way which I still have. Kevin Pritchard, Daryl Heighway, John Logan, Peter Goodwin, Bill Reid and I were amongst the first to surf most Gisborne surf spots. John was youngest in the group but he had a car so he was very popular.'*

John Logan: *'We were still surfing straight in and sticking to our favourite swimming beaches. But about the same time that the first movie arrived, so did Bob Davie and the Aussies. We suddenly found out just what could be done on waves.'*

Kevin Pritchard was renowned in the Gisborne surf circles for going out in any surf, no matter what size. *'I started surfing when I was 13. On big days at Midway I would walk out on the breakwater at Waikanae and jump in, then paddle down to Midway and wait for a whopper to surf in on. People would gather on the beach and watch. The surf life saving guys would stand on top of the army huts they used for the clubrooms, to see out the back.'* Kevin was responsible for bringing the first surf movie (*Surfing Hollow Days*) to Gisborne and it made a big impression on all the local surfers.

The early Gisborne gang surfed mainly at Waikanae, Wainui and Makarori but they did venture as far as Whangamata, Tolaga Bay and Raglan. John, Kevin and Dave all gave up surfing in the mid-60s due to work and family pressures.

Further south, Denis Quane was sharing the waves of Christchurch with Kerry McDonald, Kent Pearson, Alan Lavender, Duncan Rogers, Jimmy Wallace and the Lane brothers, Paul, Brian and Ross. One of New Zealand's first woman surfers was also amongst the Christchurch pioneers.

Bev Breward began surfing in the late 1950s at Taylor's Mistake in Christchurch. She borrowed longboards from Denis Quane and Kerry McDonald and struggled to master them in the waves. In 1960 she went on a working holiday to Australia and bought a Barry Bennett balsa Malibu board which she had freighted back to New Zealand. (Bev recalls Denis taking a mould from the board when she returned and Denis said it was

(left) Bev Breward styling on a wave during a visit to California in 1964. *'I believe I was the only woman surfing in Christchurch in the early 1960s.'*

(left) Cindy Webb, Raglan, 1964.

(below) Peter Braun at Whangamata with the balsa surfboard he acquired from Sydney, 1961. Cindy Webb: *'Peter was a member of the surf life saving club and had the first surfboard at Whangamata. Most of the surfers who thought they discovered Whangamata failed to recognise that Peter and other members of the surf life saving club had been surfing there for at least a year before them. I learned to surf on Peter's board.'*

one of the first Malibu boards he had seen.) With the lighter and more manoeuvrable board, Bev set about improving her surfing over the next few years.

Another trail blazer for women's surfing was Cindy Webb who took up the noble sport of surfing at Whangamata, aged 16. *'My introduction to surfing was in 1961 on a balsa surfboard owned by Peter Braun, one of the members of the Whangamata Surf Life Saving Club. Peter had acquired his board from Australia. It was red and near enough to 10' long. He was kind enough to lend it to me as much as I wished which was about six hours a day! I was totally devoted to learning to ride that thing but I didn't really know*

PHOTO CINDY WEBB COLLECTION

(above) **A group of surfers from Taylors Mistake, Christchurch, visiting Whangamata for Easter 1962. Peter Way is third from left, chatting to the visitors. Cindy Webb: *'They had driven all the way from Christchurch in that car – a classic surf car of the times.'***

PHOTO CINDY WEBB COLLECTION

(right) **By the summer of 1961-62, the Whangamata Surf Life Saving Club members had acquired a number of surfboards which Cindy was able to borrow. *(l to r)* Gary Marshall, Gary Gooding, Cindy Webb, Peter Braun, Bruce Bryant.**

what I was supposed to do. I presumed I should ride the white water in to shore but there were no movies or magazines around to give hints. It had no wax and was really slippery. I finally learnt to stand up and ride the white water to the beach, and after a couple of weeks I started turning a bit to the left, by accident at first, and discovered "broaching".

'One day two men appeared on the beach with surfboards. We fell upon each other as fellow members of a not-quite-yet-defined cult. They explained to me that I should be trying to catch the wave before it broke and riding the face in front of the curl. This opened up new and endless possibilities. They also informed me that I was a "goofy foot" – riding with my right foot forward. It was very exciting getting all this new information.'

It was another two years before Cindy saved up and got her own board. However, her hours of practice at Whangamata, and later Raglan, were rewarded when she enjoyed contest success in the following years.

Kick out

The arrival of lightweight boards and access to cars had caused a revolution on the beaches in New Zealand. The new breed of 'surfers' could pack up their boards and go anywhere they liked to surf. Surf life saving clubs were no longer required for storing equipment, and the patrols and loyalties were considered a hindrance to surfing by many of the new recruits.

An alternative culture of surfing developed and attracted a number of young people looking for a change from the slightly repressive society of early 1960s New Zealand. As more surfers appeared on the beaches, more were attracted to the sport and a board-building industry grew to cater for the demand.

By 1962-63, there were still only a few hundred surfers in the country but the structure was in place for the sport to take off. And on the horizon, like a storm front, the 'surf culture' of California was poised to invade New Zealand through movies and magazines.

(right) Trophy winners from the 1963 nationals: (l to r) Peter Way (Senior Men), T. White (Senior Paddle), John McDermott (Open), Phil Delaney (Team), Wayne Butt (Junior and Junior Paddle).

(left) The trophy line-up for the first New Zealand Surf Riding Championships, featuring surfboard trophies hand-made by Ted Davidson.

(below) The board lineup for the 1963 nationals, perched against the Mount Maunganui Surf Life Saving Club rooms. Surfboards were still quite an exotic sight at this time, and seeing this many together was quite remarkable.

Around 1963, a new surge of activity occurred in the industry, administration and sport of surfing. Surfing had been 'discovered', the 'pioneers' had created some infrastructure, and now the 'settlers' were arriving.

It was becoming apparent that surfing was growing at a rapid rate and that the established board makers, few that they were, could not meet the demand for new boards. New players stepped in to fill the gap and helped increase the momentum of surfing.

As the surfing population increased, crowding at popular beaches led to conflict with the surf life savers but also encouraged exploration of new, less populated breaks. Distant groups of surfers began to make contact with each other and organise visits to each other's breaks. This soon manifested itself into informal competitions and, by 1963, the first national surfing championship was held at Mount Maunganui.

The arrival of competitive surfing

Dave Walpole was a dedicated surfer and surf life saver at Mount Maunganui. He was very committed to the Mount Maunganui Surf Life Saving Club and felt that board riders should also be surf life savers – they were an integral part of the Mount. His thinking (along withthat of Jock Carson, Ted Davidson and many others) was that the more surfers there were, the more potential surf life savers there were.

Dave approached the New Zealand Surf Life Saving Association (NZSLSA) informally to suggest that a surf riders' association could be formed under the banner of NZSLSA. The idea was rejected outright and he was told in no uncertain terms that NZSLSA would not become involved with surf riders. The same antagonism that had split surf life savers and surfers in the previous three to four years was still alive and well. There was also the problem of respectability – surf life savers having it and surfers not.

Dave attempted to organise a national surfing competition in

1962, in association with the Mount Maunganui Surf Life Saving Club, but this was thwarted by the NZSLSA who were determined that anything to do with surf and national competition would be controlled by them. The competition had been intended for December of 1962 but it was abandoned.

Together with John Langlois of the Mount Maunganui Surf Life Saving Club, Dave was determined to put on a show of surfing that would demonstrate to the NZSLSA how organised and strong surfers could be. Dave realised the potential of surfing as a sport in New Zealand. (This really fanned the flames of antagonism between the surfers and surf life savers, although within both camps there were groups who were for an alliance.) New entrant to the board building scene, Atlas Woods, who had also quickly recognised the potential of surfing, donated boards as prizes.

Dave wrote to the USA, to John Severson (who was well known for his involvement in surf administration, publishing and film making in the USA, and who had stayed at Mount Maunganui during a stay in New Zealand), asking for and receiving ideas on how to run a surf competition. Ted Davidson helped with the organisation and made the trophies. For the purposes of the national competition Dave, John, Ted, Rex Woods and Dave Robinson formed the Mount Board Riders, only the third board riders club to be formed after North Reef (Takapuna) and Point (Raglan). In Auckland, where a significant number of the entrants for the first champs came from, Clive Mitchell, Phil Walker and Roger Kelly were hard at work rounding up the surfers.

The Atlas Woods New Zealand Surf Riding Championship ran over Easter weekend of 1963, and was a great success. Peter Way became the Men's Champion, Wayne Butt the Junior Champion and John McDermott became Open Men's Champion (the open category allowed non-New Zealanders to compete). There was no women's competition. Alan Godfery reported on the competition for the newspaper and there began to be strong interest in surfing around the country.

(above) The judging area and spectators for the first New Zealand Surf Riding Championships, held at Mount Maunganui, Easter 1963. The photo was taken by Dave Walpole, organiser of the competition, and his wife and son can be seen in the foreground.

(above) After the success of the first nationals, the 1964 competition was again held at Mount Maunganui. (l to r) Peter Way, Campbell Ross, Tony Bishop, John McDermott. John went on to win the title.

(right) There was a good turnout of surfers and spectators. Between heats, they danced the 'Stomp' to the music played over the loudspeakers (Liz Court in the red shirt).

Alan Godfery was a keen photographer who became friends with the early surfers and took many rolls of film during the first explorations of the coast. He told me, *'I was often asked away on the surf trips, even though I was not a surfer, because I was already selling some photos to* Surfing World *in Australia and the boys hoped they might get their picture in the magazine.'*

In the wake of a successful nationals, Dave and John Langlois decided to form a surf riders' association despite the NZSLSA. They submitted their draft constitution to NZSLSA who still would not accept an affiliation. The New Zealand Surf Riders Association (NZSRA) became an official body by mid-1963 with Dave Walpole as its first president and John Langlois as the first treasurer. Clive Mitchell became secretary and the regions were represented by Peter Way, Phil Walker, Mike Gardiner, Red (Robert) Lewton, Mike Styles and Jim Mowtell.

There was to be no reconciliation with the NZSLSA despite a folder full of correspondence. Dave Walpole: *'They even went as far as labelling the surfers who won prizes at the first nationals as "professionals" and sent letters to surf life savers warning them not to compete in surf competitions.'* Despite these teething problems, the Surf Riders' Association went from strength to strength and a national competition was held every year throughout the 1960s.

The first four nationals (1963-66) were considered, by most surfers, a wonderful opportunity to get together with their far-flung fellow enthusiasts and find out what was going on in surfing around the country. Surfers were still a rare and isolated breed – the opportunity to see each other's style and boards, and hear about new breaks, was relished. And new style was what 1963 national open class winner, John McDermott, introduced to the gathered throng.

'Hermit'

John 'Hermit' McDermott started surfing at about 13 years old on Australia's Central Coast. In 1962, he met Peter Way in Australia and Peter invited him over to New Zealand. He arrived in New Zealand in late 1962 and was picked up at the airport by

Peter and Jim Mowtell, and taken straight to Raglan.

John gave the whole surf community a surprise with the quality of his surfing. He had been surfing for some time in Australia and his experience really showed when he won the Open Men's category of the first nationals.

John deserves special mention here because the early surfers I spoke to, almost without exception, quoted him as a big influence on their surfing. He demonstrated speed, movement and style on a surfboard to a degree that hadn't been explored in New Zealand at that stage. The local surfers took up the challenge and the overall surfing standard rose quickly, as experienced at the 1964 nationals, again at Mount Maunganui. John was still ahead of the crowd, however, and as a new resident of New Zealand, he won the Senior Men's title.

Word gets out – visitors come in

As New Zealand discovered surfing, the world's surfers began to discover New Zealand. Visitors from Australia and the USA began to arrive in New Zealand, finding a country with uncrowded waves, easy work, cheap living and friendly locals. Overseas surfers were greeted with open arms as the bearers of new surfing moves, styles, clothes and boards. These visitors

John McDermott was an inspiration to local surfers with his style, speed and confidence on a board.
***(top right)* Bethells Beach, 1962.**

***(below)* John McDermott checks out one of the local home-made boards in Taranaki. John's shaping skills were soon in demand after his arrival in New Zealand.**

PHOTO ALAN GODFERY

PHOTO MIKE GARDINER

were the best, and sometimes the only, source of news from the outside surfing communities before the arrival of the movies and magazines. Peter Morse, 13-year-old grommet in 1963: *'Overseas influence was huge and any movies or mags would be devoured. Visiting surfers would have any label clothing or equipment bought or stolen from them very quickly.'*

Following in the footsteps of Bing Copeland and Rick Stoner, Americans were the main visitors from overseas in the early 60s, and included John Severson, Phil Edwards and Bud Browne. They were followed by the likes of Bruce Brown, Fred van Dyke, Bob Cooper, Sam Deikelman and 'Hiho' Silver.

First stop in New Zealand for most of these visitors from the USA was Tim Murdoch's house. Tim went to California and Hawaii nearly every year during the 1960s and the contacts he made overseas meant he played host for most American visitors coming to New Zealand.

I spoke to Bruce Brown and Fred Van Dyke and asked what it was like stepping from California and Hawaii into early New Zealand surfing.

Bruce Brown: *'I first visited New Zealand in 1961 filming for* Surfing Hollow Days. *I was travelling with Phil Edwards and we went to Australia first, then on to New Zealand. I liked to get off the beaten track for my surf movies – I tried to be different.*

'I saw very few surfers on that trip and any that were around tended to come out to see Phil surfing. Phil's surfing was miles ahead of anyone in Australia or New Zealand. The locals were happy to surf the slow rollers at the beach breaks but I was looking for points and reefs to film. We didn't get very good surf on that trip.

'I loved the New Zealand countryside and the absence of people and surfing crowds. The people were really friendly compared to the Aussies. More gentlemanly. But we were really surprised by the strong link with surf life saving. We weren't used to that. Local surfers would say to us, "Come down and have a pint at the surf club." And we'd go "Bullshit! Let's go surfing!"

'I returned in the summer 63-64 with Robert (August) and Mike (Hynson) to film The Endless Summer. *There wasn't much*

PHOTO GEOFF LOGAN, PHOTO NEWS

difference on the surf front – it was still empty and a long way behind the US. I just loved it. South Africa and New Zealand were my favourite places because of the people.

'We were always on a tight budget so we kept moving around trying to find good surf to film. There were no useful weather reports and local knowledge was limited because of the small number of surfers. We did some trout fishing as well but I just remember New Zealand as quiet, very friendly, beautiful and having empty surf.'

Fred Van Dyke: *'I met Tim Murdoch in California and he told me what a great place New Zealand was. Kennedy had just been shot, the environment was getting messed up and I just wanted to get away from the States. I decided to go to New Zealand and change my citizenship. When I arrived there, in my suit, I got asked for autographs because I sort of resembled Bobby Kennedy.*

'I stayed in New Zealand for one month in 1963-64. I travelled the country a bit on my own, and with Chip Post who was staying in New Zealand. Chip and I went to New Plymouth where Dave Littlejohn showed us around and treated us like kings.

'I remember New Zealand as having no crowds, no hassling and very friendly people. I was welcomed with open arms. I never had to worry about a place to stay or where to get a meal.

'I had some sponsorship from John Severson at Surfer Magazine *who asked me to write an article about the trip. I called it "The Time Machine". That's what New Zealand was like, going back in time. I*

(above) Judging for a local contest in Gisborne, 1964. (l to r) Des Byrne, Ian Hammon, Geoff Thompson, Bob Davie, Paul Dobson, Dave Walpole, Chip Post and Bob 'Arab' Steele. Bob Davie and Bob Steele had recently arrived in Gisborne from Australia, and Chip Post was visiting from the USA. They were the forerunners of many international surfing visitors to New Zealand during the 1960s.

PHOTO TUI WORDLEY

(above) 'Tats' Cochrane, Ahipara, Northland, 1965. Tats was notorious as one of the hard-living, scrapping, thieving Aussies. Whether these descriptions were justified or not, he certainly shows here that he was thirty years ahead of the modern surfers for tattoos and 'attitude'.

PHOTO BOB COMER

John Logan: *'The Aussies cultivated long hair, preferably blond, and wore beach baggies while we locals were still wearing Speedos and doing surf life saving. The movies and the Aussies made us realise the potential of reefs and points of which there were plenty around Gisborne.'*

(left) John McDermott, Raglan, 1963. Bob Comer: *'He's stalling prior to finding the nose and doing at least a 10-second nose ride. I was so impressed with the skills of the man that I forgot to press the shutter to record the nose ride.'*

(right) The Cronulla boys with Nigel Dwyer's Packard in Gisborne, 1964. Nigel moved to New Plymouth in 1965. Doug Hislop: *'Parties at Nigel's house, "The Castle", were legendary. Naked women were known to flee down the street and a favourite game was to kill the lights mid-party and chase unsuspecting guests around the house, giving them a quick thrashing with a pool cue when caught. Nigel got really frustrated at not being able to catch me because my hiding place was too good – I would jump onto the mantelpiece above the fireplace and stand with my back against the wall, then quickly get back to floor level before the lights came back on. I never told Nigel that.'*

PHOTO BOB COMER

PHOTO ALAN GODFERY

thought it was paradise with the surfing, fishing and farming.

'I hardly saw any surfers on the whole trip – a few in New Plymouth, a couple at Ninety Mile Beach and a couple at Piha. Surfing was still really primitive compared to the States. I did some diving and trout fishing, and I saw some big surf on the West Coast. It was a good 20-foot but Chip and I didn't go out because it was too scary with no one around.

'I've been back to New Zealand several times over the years and it is still paradise.'

As the 60s rolled on, Americans continued to visit our shores but it was Australians discovering New Zealand as a surf destination that led to an improvement in surfing and board building.

Watch out ... the Aussies are coming!

Some of the first Australian surfers to visit our country, such as Peter Troy, Terry Tumeth and Alan Dorman, returned to their home beaches in Sydney with stories of New Zealand's empty waves, easy life and cheap icecream. Gradually, the flow of visitors from Australia increased and with them came a superior level of surfing skill, a good history and knowledge of board building, and an ability to get by on one's wits that surprised and shocked many of the local surfers.

John McDermott arrived close on the heels of those first Aussie visitors. Although only 17 years old when he arrived in

Auckland, in late 1962, John was already a proficient surfer and shaper. He lived in Auckland for about three years, hanging out, surfing and working with Peter Way. He also did some shaping for Atlas Woods before moving to Christchurch in 1966, where he worked for Denis Quane. His surfing skills were far ahead of the locals and he is mentioned by all the early surfers as a huge influence on the surfing of the times.

Mike Gardiner, one of North Piha's first surfers and a contemporary of Peter Way, says he spent a lot of time surfing with visiting Australians who had made it to Piha. *'I liked to surf with the Aussie guys because their surfing was so good. You could learn a lot by watching them, and they were pretty good fun to travel with – pretty wild.'*

Being 'pretty wild' seems to have been a feature of the visitors from Australia. They had several years' experience of living on very little money and begging, borrowing or stealing to support a surfing lifestyle. When they brought this same attitude to New Zealand, the locals were surprised to say the least.

Following is a selection of the comments offered with respect to the early Aussie visitors:

'Everyone used to leave their cars unlocked at The Point until the Aussies arrived. Straight away, anything that wasn't bolted down was flogged. They changed the mood out there quite quickly. Their level of thievery was a real eye-opener for us.'

'The Aussies amazed me with their shoplifting. They would go into a dairy and come out with their pockets full! It was quite staggering.'

PHOTO GEOFF LOGAN, PHOTO NEWS

(far left, l to r) **Chip Post and Fred Van Dyke were early visitors to New Zealand from the USA. Fred:** *'We hardly saw any surfers on the whole trip – a few in New Plymouth, a couple at Ninety Mile Beach and a couple at Piha. Surfing was still really primitive compared to the States. I did some diving and trout fishing, and I saw some big surf on the West Coast. It was a good 20-foot but Chip and I didn't go out because it was too scary with no one around.'*

PHOTO RICK BRADLEY

The Australians made a big impact in New Zealand. Their skills were several years ahead of most local surfers. *(above)* **Russell Hughes on the nose at Whangamata, 1964.** **Andy McAlpine:** *'Russell was one of the first to "climb and drop" on waves – a preview of short board moves.'*

(left) **Alan Dorman, Gisborne, 1964.**

Mike Gardiner: *'In Auckland, I was hired to deliver a 70' motor launch that had a writ on it. On arrival at Sydney, I would be paid £1000, a small fortune in those days. Bob Davie, 'Arab' Steele, Paul von Zalinski and I boarded the boat, removed the writ from the mast and motored out of the harbour. We had no experience, no navigational ability, no life rafts and scarcely enough supplies. "Go to the top of the North Island and turn left" were the instructions. We nearly hit the Three Kings islands when we encountered a gale at the top of the North Island, only realising the next day that we had passed between the islands during the night. We found Sydney Harbour purely by luck just before running out of fuel and food.'*
(right, l to r) **Bob Davie, Paul von Zalinski and Mike Gardiner.**
(below right) **Bob Steele at the helm.**
(below left) **Paul von Zalinski attempts to understand how a sextant works.**

PHOTO MIKE GARDINER

PHOTO MIKE GARDINER

PHOTO MIKE GARDINER

'The influx of Australian surfers really changed the nature of surfing in New Zealand. The less financial visitors introduced a level of thieving and scamming that was an eye-opener to the New Zealanders. Over a short period of time, it became unsafe to leave cars unlocked or possessions lying on the beach.

'Aussie visitors would travel from town to town having a 21st birthday at each place and collecting presents; they would sell insured boards and then collect the insurance; and at the basic level, they would shoplift on a scale and frequency that locals found hard to believe. To be charitable, they were very good at surviving on minimal money.

'The positive aspect of the Australian influx was their effect on surfing in New Zealand. We had been late starters and now, suddenly, surfers with several years' experience, like Hermit (John McDermott) were arriving in the country and tearing up the waves. Locals suddenly became aware of just what could be done on a surfboard.'

Most of the Aussies who caused strife were kept in line by local 'enforcers' and left the country after a short time. The rest of the Australian surfers impressed with their skills in the surf and in board making. Several, such as John McDermott, Bob Davie and Nigel Dwyer, stayed on to have a big influence on surfing in New Zealand.

Bob Davie arrived in Auckland in 1963 along with travelling companion 'Arab' Steel. From talking to other surfers who had visited New Zealand and reading a magazine article about the country, Bob knew there were uncrowded waves and that the surfing industry was in its infancy. His aim was to come to New Zealand and build enough surfboards to finance a prolonged surfing holiday.

Bob has subsequently been a New Zealand senior surf champion (1965) and run a string of board factories from Gisborne to Mount Maunganui to Auckland. He has been in the forefront of New Zealand's surf scene since 1963 and been instrumental in keeping New Zealand's surfers up to date with international standards and trends. He trained numerous shapers, many of whom have gone on to successful careers of their own, such as Alan Byrne and Rodney Dahlberg. Bob also got involved in the club and administrative side of surfing and was a strong competitor for the Bay Surfers Club. He is one of the few originators of surfing in New Zealand who has remained totally involved in the sport, right up to the present day.

Nigel Dwyer arrived in Gisborne, in 1965, with a group of fellow Cronulla surfers – John Gittens, Graeme Gibson, Bob (Stud) Ayres, John (LT) Finn, Keith Paul, John Bonas and Ken Wensenias. They were looking for their only contact in New Zealand, fellow Cronulla surfer Bob Davie.

Nigel became notorious in Gisborne for his surfing skills, his glassing skills and for the enormous 1938 Packard in which he and his Aussie travelling partners would roar around the country raising hell, both in and out of the water. Nigel is adamant that most of the Aussies in New Zealand were honest and hard working, and that their bad reputation was undeserved.

Nigel worked as a glasser with both Bob Davie and Roger Land and introduced them to the 'squeegee' for working the resin. They had been using rollers and paint brushes but the squeegee gave a vastly better finish. Bob Davie: *'Nigel was a good surfer and had a strong influence on the current styles. He was responsible for surfing being taken more seriously around Gisborne. He was also a top quality glasser and really helped us improve the boards we were making.'*

Nigel drove to New Plymouth for the 1965 nationals. While there he met Dave Littlejohn who approached Nigel about making boards in New Plymouth. This partnership resulted in the formation of Del Surfboards in an old house in New Plymouth. Nigel used mainly Australian shapers and glassers over the following years until local workers had learned the necessary skills. This habit of importing the shaping skills meant that Del Surfboards was quite influential on local shapers.

Del faced the same dilemma as all the board builders in the 60s, of trying to get good quality resin and fibreglass in bulk, without having to pay the earth. The market in New Zealand was controlled by AC Hatrix Limited who had the necessary import

licences to get the materials. Import licences were almost impossible to get hold of so the options were limited. Even if a factory got an import licence, they had to get the overseas funds to pay for the material, another difficult task in the highly controlled economic environment of the 60s. By exporting some boards to South Africa, Del managed to get the all important foreign currency they needed to import resin from Brian Jackson in Sydney.

Del used a number of 'beach agents' around the country – surfers who would take orders from others at the beach, then mail the order to Del. One of his best beach agents was Gary McCormick who would take orders for boards from the surfers at Titahi Bay and surrounds. Doug Hislop took orders for Del boards when he was in Gisborne and Rick Bradley took care of the Hamilton agency.

As the 60s progressed, Nigel became president of the Cape Board Riders Club and became involved with the NZSRA. He created the Del International Trophy for the winner of a surf-off between the top two surfers from the juniors, seniors and open events at the national surf champs. (This was to try and overcome any comments relating to the best surfers not getting to surf against each other because of the categories.) He has gone from strength to strength as the years have gone by and his contribution to New Zealand surfing continues to this day.

The influence of the Australians was short and sharp on New Zealand in the early 60s. On the negative side, a number of the visitors caused a culture of honesty and courtesy that existed in the New Zealand surfing community to be replaced by suspicion and caution when dealing with other surfers. It is worth noting that the New Zealanders were apparently very quick to learn these lessons from the Aussies and apply them to their own travels in Australia.

On the positive side, the Australians brought experience and skills in surf riding and board building that New Zealanders had not seen. They were responsible for a sudden leap forward in surfing ability and board construction that we needed in order to catch up with the rest of the world.

(above) **'Pogo' Watson, New Plymouth, 1963. Dave Littlejohn:** *'This is an Aussie called 'Pogo' Watson who was a regular visitor. He was an airline steward and could fly over for about £10. This photo was taken on his wedding day which he chose to celebrate in New Zealand. He didn't marry the surfboard.'*

The new board builders

From 1963, a new wave of surf enthusiasts began building boards. Some had been surfing a few years and saw it as a good way to finance the lifestyle, while others, who were new to surfing, saw it as a cheap way to enter the sport. And one new entrant to the board market, Atlas Woods Surfboards, did so purely for business reasons, having successfully predicted that surfing would take off in New Zealand.

(right) **Atlas Woods** *were* **number one but there was serious competition from some of the other board manufacturers. To stay ahead of the pack, Atlas used marketing strategies such as having New Zealand champion, Wayne Parkes, on their team.**

Wayne Parkes Surfing at Mangawai Heads.

Wayne Parkes, Designer and Shaper. N.Z. Champ.

Wayne and Glen Kelly discussing shapes.

Tony Ogilvy, Shaper and leading Junior Surfer.

Steve King, Atlas/Woods Manager

New Zealand's No. 1 Innovators
Wayne Parkes and Atlas/Woods

The Innovators: Wayne Parkes and Atlas/Woods. A team dedicated to giving you the board that fulfils your creative demands. New shape pin tails, square tails and trackers. Flat or V-bottom. Lighter boards. Featuring all the revolutionary advances that make your old board obsolete, your new board No. 1. Such as the exclusive Removable bolt-on fins in transparent colours, opaque black or clear I.P.C.*

Wayne Parkes and our other top shapers get involved with your board requirements. They create and shape in one of the most progressive factories in the country. They will design to your own specifications, at no extra cost.

Wayne Parkes, No. 1 shaper, knows where he is going and

what he is doing. His qualifications: 3 times winner of the N.Z. Senior title. Experienced in surf the world over, including Hawaii, Australia, California. N.Z. representative in the World Champs. at Puerto Rico.

Get with what's happening. An Atlas/Woods innovation is your answer to creative surfing. See your local Atlas/Woods Board Shop or write to us. *Indestructible Plastic Compound

Atlas/Woods, Wairau Road, Takapuna, AUCKLAND, 9.
Atlas/Woods Surf Shop, P.O. Box 3798, AUCKLAND, 1.
Ph: 32·985 or 493·987

ATLAS/WOODS

ATLAS WOODS SURFBOARDS

NG NEW ZEALAND · 4

Atlas Woods Surfboards

Alan Mitchell ran the Atlas Trading Company which imported sports goods into New Zealand. Recognising the potential of the surfing craze in the early 60s, Alan had tried to get import licences for boards or blanks. However, as every other board manufacturer in New Zealand discovered, the licences were impossible to get, so he imported the expertise instead.

He had tried blowing his own foam but hadn't been able to achieve the standard necessary for quality surfboard production. Alan travelled to Australia, where the surfboard industry was firmly established, and asked around for the best source of blanks. He was directed to Gordon Woods. After some discussion and inspection of the product, they came to an agreement whereby Gordon sent a mould (expensive but vital to the production of a good blank) to New Zealand. He then came over to show Alan how to make the blanks and where to source the base materials (which Alan could get import licences for). For this, Gordon received a royalty for each board made and his name on the product, thus, Atlas Woods.

In 1963, Gordon Woods arrived in New Zealand the same day as the mould. It was unloaded and transported to the basement of a building on the corner of Emily Place and Fort Street, in Auckland City, and Atlas Woods had blown its first blank by the next day.

Alan blew the blanks himself in those early years and shudders now to think of the conditions in that basement – a low roof, full of fumes and a floor covered with foam and resin sludge. Ably assisting during this set-up phase was George Tomlin, a handyman in the truest sense, epitomised by his developing into a good shaper for Atlas Woods. Alan described George as the man who could make his ideas come into being.

The boards immediately sold as fast as they could produce them and, within a year, Alan had hired Ken Clark. George Tomlin taught Ken how to glass and shape boards.

The blanks that Atlas Woods produced were of sufficiently superior quality that many backyard board makers gave up

continued on page 50

Bob Davie

'Came for a holiday and ended up staying.'

Bob is such a feature of New Zealand surfing that it is easy to forget that he originally came to New Zealand from Sydney, in 1963, for a working holiday. When I went to see him at his house in Whangamata, he had just done a television appearance for one of the local travel shows, had recently completed an interview for a local surf video and had been contacted several times in the previous year for his opinion on various matters to do with surfing in New Zealand. The phone continued to ring during my visit and I realised that Bob still had his finger well and truly on the pulse of surfing in our country – and that was winter!

So how did an Aussie import come to be an authority on surfing in New Zealand?

In the early 60s, Bob was looking for some surf adventure outside Australia and, after seeing an article about New Zealand in a magazine, he decided it was worth a visit. He arrived in Auckland, late 1963, with travelling companion Bob 'Arab' Steel. They headed straight out to Piha where they met Peter Byers and Peter Way, both of whom recommended a visit to Raglan. The guys had brought a car with them so they unloaded it from the ship and drove to Raglan that same night.

'I don't know why we brought a car with us – maybe we didn't

(below) **Bob at Makarori Point, Gisborne, 1964. A favourite break and a favourite time of his life.**

PHOTO RICK BRADLEY

PHOTO GEOFF LOGAN, PHOTO NEWS

(above, l to r) **Peter Goodwin and Bob Davie at the 1964 nationals, Mount Maunganui.**

think they would have any in New Zealand. We missed Manu Bay in the dark and parked at Whale Bay. When we woke up in the morning, the surf was breaking right through from Indicators to Whale Bay and, of course, no one out. We paddled out and caught some monsters but eventually lost our boards [pre-legrope days] *and washed up on the rocks. We drove into town to get some breakfast and passed Manu Bay on the way ... things looked pretty good and a lot more manageable. We stayed on and surfed Raglan for a few more days, without seeing any other surfers, before returning to Auckland. Not a bad way to start a trip we thought.'*

Bob and Arab did a bit of sanding for Peter Way before setting up a small board factory in Point Chevalier using blanks blown by Peter Byers. Bob hadn't shaped boards before but had watched Arab doing repairs and glassing at Clive Jackson Surfboards in Cronulla, Sydney. He had also done some ding repairs of his own so they started making their own boards. Bob had originally come to New Zealand with the intention of making boards to fund a prolonged surfing holiday, and had even imported a mould he had made beforehand in Sydney.

Towards the end of 1963, Bob and Arab left Auckland to search for surf again. They spent about four months in New Plymouth surfing with Mike Gardiner. Once again, there were few other surfers around and a lot of good surf, even if a bit cold without wetsuits. To keep the bank balance intact, they took on possum hunting in Taupo (hence the long-term nickname of 'Possum' Davie).

At the start of 1964, Bob and Arab drove to Gisborne where they immediately felt comfortable with the proximity of the beach and the abundant surf. They started making boards under the Bob Davies Surfboards name and things quickly took off. Bob Davies Surfboards sold about 90% of the boards ridden in Gisborne, Hawkes Bay and the surrounding areas. The boards gained attention for being significantly shorter than the norm (9'6" versus 10' plus) and were adopted by many of the top surfers of the time, including Alan Byrne, Wayne Parkes (before his move to Atlas Woods) and the Patty twins of Gisborne.

Bob's reputation was further enhanced in 1965 when he won the national title at New Plymouth. Adding to the stature of his board building factory was a visit, in 1966, by Bob McTavish who came over from Australia to shape for Bob Davies Surfboards for four months.

Alan Byrne: *'I would like to emphasise how important I think Bob Davie was for surfing in New Zealand, not only because of the skills he had but also because he kept attracting a steady flow of top board builders and surfers to Gisborne, such as Russell Hughes, Keith Paull and Bob McTavish. They learnt things in New Zealand and went back to influence Australia. Bob was always current and experimental, and kept us up to date with the rest of the world.'*

It was an exciting time for surfing in Gisborne as locations such as The Island and Mahia were just being discovered. Surfers were welcomed at all the breaks, being sources of new information, styles and board design. There were plenty of waves for everyone and the surfing community quickly became a strong one. Bob remembers this as one of the best times of his life.

In 1966, Bob closed up shop in Gisborne and opened a board factory at Mount Maunganui which seemed an obvious choice for expansion. It was closer to a number of important surf breaks, including Coromandel and Raglan, and closer to Auckland, another potential area of expansion. At the height of the 1966-67 summer season at Mount Maunganui, they were selling 40 boards a week.

In 1967-68, Bob opened a factory in Auckland in partnership with Mike Court (the same premises that Wayne Parkes Surfboards uses today). He also opened small factories at Waihi Beach and Whangamata. At one point, Bob employed 25 staff in six different shops. The factory at Mount Maunganui was the base for operations and from there Bob would refine his shaping ideas and then travel to the other factories to give instruction. The Mount factory also blew all the blanks for the other factories so it was quite a busy operation.

The problem was that it got too busy and Bob found that the business allowed no time for surfing which was still very important to him. The very things which had appealed to him about surfing originally, such as leaving all your worries behind on the beach, no longer held true – the surf was full of people who were waiting for their new boards. So, in 1970, he simply closed the factory at Mount Maunganui and sold off the rest of his business. He bought a shop in the main street of Whangamata, and a house on four acres just out of town.

Those four acres are now covered in lush bush, full of native birds, and the house is a sun-filled haven away from what can sometimes be a maddening Whangamata township. Bob shapes a few boards in a shed in the garden and runs his business from home as much as possible.

Since 1970, Bob has been involved in Saltwater Surfboards, Lipsticks and now, Bob Davies Surfboards again. He runs the surf shop, Whangamata Surfboards, and surfing is still a passion. Since 1963, he has been surfer, shaper, retailer and administrator, and his contribution to the sport is one of the strongest in New Zealand surfing history.

(right) **An advertisement for Bob Davie Surfboards from 1970. It is a good sample of the hippy style that was popular, and the new board shapes can just be made out.**

(below) **Bob surfing Waikanae Beach in his early days at Gisborne, 1964.**

PHOTO GRAY CLAPHAM COLLECTION

(above) Steve King, Crescent Heads, Australia, 1965. 'I started at Atlas Woods as a glasser then became manager. We had the best factory – even in those days it had an extraction system better than most have now. At one point we had a really good crew of craftsmen – Wayne shaping, the Tinkler brothers shaping and glassing, Dave Carter doing the colours and finishing, Pete Cogan glassing, Phil Jamisen doing airbrush and shaping, and Tony Ogilvy learning to shape.'

trying to blow their own and instead purchased them from Atlas Woods. This came back to haunt Alan to some degree when those same board makers became successful enough to undermine Atlas Woods' board sales in the late 1960s. Atlas Woods also began making wetsuits at the Emily Place factory and their success placed a real strain on the available space and facilities.

Alan Mitchell already had an established sports goods wholesale business, with a team of sales representatives, and was perfectly positioned to get Atlas Woods boards into the mainstream sports stores and department stores. This was the trump card that allowed Atlas Woods to outsell its competitors.

By the end of 1966, demand was so strong that Alan built a new factory in Wairau Road, on the North Shore of Auckland. The factory was specifically built to cater for the rise in custom surfboard production. Staff numbers at Wairau Road were

(right) An Advertisement for Atlas Woods Surfboards from 1965-66.

increased to approximately 12, including 4-5 shapers, one of whom was New Zealand's new surfing champion, Wayne Parkes.

Atlas Woods would produce mainly production boards over winter and then custom boards throughout summer. After the move in 1966, the factory was making about 1500 boards a year at Wairau Road, and they were still selling as fast as they could make them. They even exported surfboards to Japan during the late 1960s.

Steve King: 'I started at Atlas Woods as a glasser then became manager. We had the best factory – even in those days it had an extraction system better than most have now. At one point we had a really good crew of craftsmen – Wayne shaping, the Tinkler brothers shaping and glassing, Dave Carter doing the colours and finishing, Pete Cogan glassing, Phil Jamisen doing airbrush and Tony Ogilvy learning to shape.'

Throughout the sixties, Atlas Woods were involved in sponsoring regional and national surfing competitions and made every effort to keep their company at the top of the surfboard industry. Alan Mitchell: 'We used all the tools we could muster, such as employing the leading surfers of the time, sponsoring the main events and making sure our products were seen and available at all the beaches. We opened our own sports stores, Sportways, just to be able to keep in touch with what was happening in the retail sector. Overseas surfers, such as Nat Young, were invited to New Zealand to promote Atlas Woods boards and surfing in general. We always felt we were one step ahead of the competition. Our forte was good marketing and tight budget control. We were much more corporate than the other board makers and were in the industry for business reasons rather than a love of surfing.'

In the early 1970s, when the initial wave of enthusiasm for surfing had been ridden and it became harder to make money from building surfboards, Atlas Woods closed its doors and the Mitchells moved onto new projects such as surf clothing, wetsuits, skateboards and windsurfers. Alan stresses that Atlas Woods was primarily a marketing company, in the modern sense of the word, and that they were selling surfing.

Peter Way

Peter financed a prolonged surfing life by board building, and sold boards throughout the country. He was not known as one of the innovators in the board building industry but his sales were enhanced by his big reputation both in and out of the water. Grommets loved to be part of the Peter Way legend.

It was 1963-64 when Peter began building boards in his parents' backyard in Sandringham, Auckland, using blanks supplied by Peter Byers. John McDermott was fresh off the plane from Australia and was shaping for Peter. Peter Way Surfboards worked from the backyard, between surfs, for about three years before taking over Ken Clark's surf shop in Albany in 1967.

Peter's dad died in 1968 and he inherited his father's debts which made life very difficult for a few years. The shop in Albany burnt down and Peter moved to new premises in Barrys Point Road (home to over a dozen different surf shops over the years) on Auckland's North Shore.

In the late 60s, Peter went into partnership with Dave Jackman and opened Jackman Way Surfboards, again in Barrys Point Road. This partnership lasted a couple of years before Peter departed for New Plymouth to surf and disappear for a while. He loved his time in New Plymouth but eventually, in 1976, left for the waves and climate of Australia's Gold Coast and only returned to New Zealand to attend the North Piha Surf Life Saving reunion in January 2000.

Frank Wilkin

As previously mentioned, Frank began building boards in the basement of his parents' house in 1961. He was producing pop-out boards under the name Kahuna, and custom boards under the name Frank Wilkin Surfboards. His parents' house took a fair amount of punishment over the years as the beams bore the weight of the moulds, and the house filled with foam dust and resin fumes. The boards were bought as fast as they could be made and the basement surfboard factory was producing 30-40 boards per week at its peak in 1965-66.

PHOTO NIGEL DWYER COLLECTION

(left, l to r) Nigel Dwyer and Peter Way showing great enthusiasm for their work, New Plymouth, 1969.

FOR YOUR NEXT CUSTOM SURFBOARD

DEAL DIRECT WITH ME

NO "MR INBETWEEN"

Seven years of board-riding experience in New Zealand and overseas

PETER WAY custom surfboard

SCOOP !!!

WRITE FOR FREE PRICE LIST AND DECAL

Nylon Fins as advertised overseas AVAILABLE NOW

PETER WAY SURFBOARDS
23 Goring Road,
Sandringham,
AUCKLAND

(left) A 1965 advertisement for Peter Way Surfboards which was still based in the backyard of Peter's parents' house in Sandringham, Auckland.

CUSTOM SURFBOARDS OF QUALITY BY SKILLED CRAFTSMEN COMBINING BEAUTY WITH PRECISION, PERFORMANCE AND RUGGED DURABILITY — THE REST IS UP TO YOU...

(above) Dunlop advertisement from 1966. Dunlop boards were pop-outs produced by Frank Wilkin. Sportex had contracted Frank to produce his Kahuna boards for them but Sportex was bought out by Dunlop who chose to use the Dunlop name for the boards.

In 1964, a sports wholesale company, Sportex, approached Frank to produce surfboards for them. They wanted pop-outs only and as many as Frank could produce. He signed a 3-year contract with them and swung into full production of the Kahuna boards. In 1966, Dunlop bought out Sportex and moved Frank's operation to larger premises, then larger premises again.

Dunlop sent Frank to Australia to check on board production there but the only thing he felt he lacked was the quality finishing resins. In all other aspects of board building, Frank felt that New Zealand was a match for Australia.

Dunlop boards were the only brand that competed with Atlas Woods in the mainstream market of sports stores and department stores. Dunlop attempted to emulate the success of Atlas Woods by using their business skills to market their surfboards but they arrived a bit too late on the scene. Within 18 months, the market for pop-out boards declined, as custom boards took over, and Dunlop closed the surfboard operation.

Frank had experimented with shorter boards and twin fins, and liked to do his own shaping, taking local conditions into account. However, he missed the short board revolution that arrived in the late 60s, as Dunlop had moved him into a new area of the business by then.

Frank describes himself as an average surfer who loved the sport but never took to the road in the same way that some of his contemporaries did. He made occasional surf trips to Raglan and the other main surf beaches of the time, but spent most of his time surfing at Piha and concentrating on trying to perfect his surfboard business.

Roger Land

Roger got his first taste of surfing at Mount Maunganui during the summer of 1961-62. Roger borrowed a board from a local surfer and although he wasn't instantly successful as a surfer, he was smitten by the surfing bug.

He built his own surfboard in his parents' backyard in Auckland, using a block of polystyrene from a local insulation company. Although he can't remember how he found out, Roger knew that he had to put a protective layer between the foam and resin so that the resin would not be dissolved. He covered the polystyrene blank with a sheet and Arolite glue but unfortunately, as the glue dried, the shrinkage wrecked the blank and he had to start again. Roger tried Acropol acrylic paint on the next attempt and he was much more successful. With a home-made Roland (ROgerLAND) sticker and laminated wooden fin, his first board looked very impressive. (A professional, good-looking finish was something that Roger maintained throughout his board building career.)

Roger surfed as much as possible during the next few years, and he worked hard on his board building. Some time was spent in the East Coast Bays of Auckland, building boards and surfing with Bill Ebdale and Bob McNabb.

In 1963-64, Roger moved to Hamilton and set up a board factory to supply the Raglan surfers. He stayed in Hamilton for 18 months before moving his business to Gisborne in 1964-65. This put him into competition with Bob Davie who had

(right) Roger Land at work in his Hamilton factory, 1965. *(inset)* 'I remember building a board for Wayne Parkes in 1963 that was 8'8" x 21", weighed 26 pounds and was red with a balsa/redwood stringer. That was a small and light board for those years but Wayne was a pretty small guy in 1963, as the order shows.'

enjoyed pretty much exclusive rights to board sales in Gisborne up until that time. Although there was a rivalry, Roger admits a respect for Bob's designs. *'Bob was more aggressive in terms of shaping and pushed the design limits more than I did. I made well-shaped, good looking boards and I sold on that basis.'* Nigel Dwyer worked with Roger, as a glasser, during this period.

Roger moved back to Hamilton and a new factory in 1965, and was soon producing up to 25 boards per week. A network of agents was established in areas that included Wellington, Tokoroa, Whangarei and Mount Maunganui, and agents began to approach Roger for boards. The business really took off but it led to cash flow problems. These were alleviated when Kevin Brightwell invested in the business but Roger immediately felt his creative spirit being dampened by an outsider's financial considerations. He sold out to Kevin at the end of 1965 and Kevin changed the name of the boards from Roger Land Surfboards to simply Land. (The business foundered after Kevin opened another factory in Frankton to produce production boards for Auckland sports wholesaler Britwyn. The Britwyn boards were shaped by Don Wilson and finished by Bob Comer.)

Roger began working on fibreglass boats in Rotorua before being coaxed back to the surfboard industry by Bob Davie. *'I would work on boats during the week in Rotorua then drive to the Mount to shape surfboards in the weekend. I moved to Mount Maunganui to work fulltime for Bob in 1967. I experienced the beginning of the "short board revolution" and helped teach Rodney Dahlberg to shape.'*

Roger and his wife departed for Hawaii at the end of 1968, and he worked overseas as a shaper until his return to New Zealand in 1971.

Rodney Davidson

In 1963, Rodney started surfing at Auckland's Takapuna Beach when he was 19 years old. He and Ken Pedersen, Dewey Lock and Dave Barker were amongst the first surfers at Takapuna. They would borrow boards and surf on anything they could get

Cowbunga...

He's got his toes where they should be, over a

RODNEY DAVIDSON SURFBOARD

SURF BOARDS by *Rodney Davidson*

Call or write
RODNEY DAVIDSON
46 King Edward Ave.,
Bayswater, Auckland.
Phone **70-946**

(above) A 1965 advertisement for Rodney Davidson Surfboards from New Zealand's first surf magazine.

(left) Rodney Davidson on his way to winning a North Reef club contest at Waipu, Northland, 1966.

their hands on.

Rodney built his first board in a shed at the back of his parents' property in Bayswater, Auckland. He got his instructions on how to build a board after talking to Clive Mitchell and Malcolm Strong who came to Takapuna for a storm surf and brought polystyrene boards with them. Rodney based his first design on the boards he saw that day.

Rodney worked from the shed for a year before starting his first board building business at Kings Store, on Auckland's North Shore, in 1963/64. He spent two years there before moving to a new factory in Barry's Point Road (that road again), Takapuna. He stayed for three years and personally built over 1000 surfboards (many of which are still around) using blanks sourced from Denis Quane and Dave Jackman.

He surfed a lot at Pakiri, Bethells and Whangamata but

(right) **Ted Davidson at work in his original joinery factory where he first began building boards, Tauranga, 1963.**

PHOTO TED DAVIDSON

travelled all over between Spirits Bay and Gisborne. Rodney remembers being one of the first to surf at Whangamata and considers it to be one of his favourite surf breaks. He was a member of North Reef Board Riders' Club and entered a few competitions for the fun of it, and for the social interaction with other surfers.

A chance call into a boat building factory to help out on a boat building project lead Rodney back to an earlier passion for ocean yacht racing. The surfboard business had become too competitive and he took the opportunity to move to the USA for two fantastic years of yacht racing and cruising. As the factory was pretty much Rodney, a couple of racks and an electric planer, it was easy to close up and move on.

Ted Davidson

Around 1961, Ted was advised by his doctor to leave the joinery factory in which he was working and get outdoors. Bill Foster of the Mount Maunganui Surf Life Saving Club, of which Ted was already a member, suggested that Ted try surfing. Bill had a board that had been built by Campbell Ross and it was on this board that Ted had his first go. He paddled out to the blow hole, at the main beach of Mount Maunganui, turned and caught a wave, and managed to stand up and ride it to the beach on his very first attempt. He was sold on the idea.

Ted decided that the easiest way to get a board was to build his own. He asked around for advice, and there was sufficient information getting to the Mount from the board builders in Hamilton for him to establish what materials he needed and where to get them. He got a piece of insulation foam for the core and went to Epiglass in Auckland for advice on resin. While most of the board builders at the time were using polyester resin, Epiglass suggested epoxy resin and catalyst DT. This meant that no protective barrier was required between foam and resin, and a lighter board could be built.

Ted's first effort was a 9'6" board with a home-made Marlin logo. Inspired by this first success, he started to make more boards and used the name Ted Davidson Custom Surfboards, on which he put a wave logo. In 1962, Ted started a business called Marine Sports which incorporated a surfboard factory, joinery factory and retail shop for surfing, boating, sailing, diving and water skiing equipment.

After the 1964 nationals at the Mount, Ted secured the agency for Atlas Woods Surfboards for the whole of the Bay of Plenty. This was on the condition that he gave up making his own boards. He sold boards from his Marine Sports shop in Tauranga and, for two years, Ted travelled to the A & P shows, throughout the Bay of Plenty, setting up displays and selling boards. He also travelled to other parts of New Zealand that Atlas Woods had not reached and, while in Southland, became a foundation member of the South Coast Board Riders' Club (he had his best surf ever at a bay in Southland).

Ted also had a full set of John Severson surf movies which he took on the road with him (through association with Tim Murdoch) and showed at clubs and halls around the country.

Business was so successful between 1964 and 1966 that in order to fulfil demand, Ted took on the Dunlop agency and eventually had to start making his own boards again. This was at a time when Bob Davies Surfboards, just over the water at Mount Maunganui, was also selling 40 boards a week during summer.

Having to send boards to Dunedin on the plane led to Ted's first experiment with shorter boards. *'The DC3 lockers could fit 10' boards but when Air New Zealand converted to Friendship aircraft, the lockers would only fit 9' boards, so I did a run of 9' boards. The boards went so well that the guys down south never went back to the longer boards.'*

Ted started a board hire business on the main beach at Mount Maunganui and ran it for three summers between 1966-68. It was very successful to begin with but took a fair amount of time to run. The Atlas agency wound down and by 1968 Ted was looking for a new line of business. He sold Marine Sports in order to buy a motor camp at Mount Maunganui. The board hire business was getting out of hand unless Ted ran it himself, which the new motor

(left) **An advertisement for Ted Davidson's Marine Sports Centre from 1965.** *'I went to see Bronco Branch of Bronco's Sports Store, in Tauranga, and asked if I could buy a surfboard. Bronco made a reply to the effect that he wouldn't be getting involved in a sport full of long-haired layabouts. He later approached Atlas Woods to enquire about selling their boards in Tauranga, only to be informed that I was the sole agent for the Bay of Plenty, something I never let him forget even though we remained good friends.'*
Ted would show his movies every Friday at the Marine Sports shop and was guaranteed an audience, even though they had seen the movies dozens of times before.

camp did not allow, so he closed that down too, ending a busy seven-year career in surfing. Ted continued to surf for some time but has only built one board since 1968, which was for his son.

Ken Clark

Ken started surfing in 1962, as a 23-year-old, around Takapuna and Orewa. His friends Doug Lamb and Ross Edmonson saw pictures of surfing and decided to try it out. Ken says he nearly drowned three times learning to surf and once had to be hauled from the water by the surf life savers at Piha.

Ken's first board was self-built using insulation foam, and shaped using pictures from a surf magazine. Someone had told Ken to coat the foam with PVA glue, and he got the fibreglass and resin from the local hardware shop where Doug Lamb worked. It lasted a few months until it broke in half while Doug was surfing on it at Piha.

Ken bought a new blank and set straight to work on a new board. It broke in half three weeks later so he stripped the glass off, cut the blank in half longways and glued it back together with a stringer, as he should have done the first time. He then reglassed the board and got a year's worth of pleasure from it

PHOTO MIKE McGLYNN

(above) **A 'super board' made by Ted Davidson to promote the surfboards he sold at A&P shows. Here it is held by Mike McGlynn** *(left)* **and friends from Paekakariki. Mount Maunganui, 1967.**

(above) North Reef at Takapuna Beach, Auckland, 1969. Ken Clark was working as a labourer on the building site for the Mon Desir Hotel at Takapuna in 1963. 'I had nearly been fired for being late three days in a row due to perfect, empty surf on North Reef which was impossible to resist. I decided that a job in the surf industry would be much more in keeping with my new lifestyle so I pestered Atlas Woods incessantly until Alan Mitchell gave me a job late in 1963.'
North Reef also lent its name to New Zealand's first surf riders' club, North Reef Board Club, which was based at Takapuna, Auckland.

before selling it and buying an Atlas Woods.

Ken was working as a labourer but decided that a job in the surf industry would be much more in keeping with his new lifestyle. He pestered Atlas Woods incessantly until Alan Mitchell gave him a job late in 1963. He started at the bottom of the ladder, wet and drying the boards (soon found to be unnecessary) after the first glass coat. He worked his way up to shaping, learning a lot from his foreman George Tomlin. He remembers a series of young American surfers coming through the factory, supposedly being experienced shapers but, in fact, being unable to shape at all and hoping to get a job to fund their trip to New Zealand.

Wayne Parkes: 'Ken was a tireless worker who used to sacrifice holidays to keep the production line rolling'. After 2-3 years with Atlas Woods Ken decided to open his own shop just north of Auckland on State Highway One. Unfortunately, his opening coincided with the first oil shortage of the 60s and he couldn't get resin locally, and had no overseas funds to purchase it offshore. The shop lasted for six months before he quit it and Peter Way took over.

In 1965, Ken got a job with Frank Wilkin at Dunlop Surfboards. Ken was hired as a glasser and sander on piece-work rates. He worked really hard and made good money but within nine months the boards had stopped selling because the designs were not keeping pace with the changes going on in surfing.

Ken took on glassing work at home for Peter Way and Nev Hines, and still made some boards of his own. His own boards were under the Ken Clark label which featured a black diamond with the ends cut off and crossed surfboards. 'I remember, after one particularly long evening working with the fumes and dust of the boards, I sat down in the lounge and suddenly found I couldn't move at all. I was completely paralysed and stuck in the chair for over an hour until the effects finally wore off.'

Ken moved into other work after that and, coupled with a surfing accident that broke his jaw and eight teeth, he left surfing behind in the 1970s.

Dave Jackman

Dave moved to Auckland, from Sydney, with his New Zealand-born wife in 1963-64. He was already a surf legend having competed in Australia and Hawaii, surfed all the notable big wave locations such as Sunset Beach and Waimea Bay, and had ridden a huge wave on an outer reef off Queenscliff in Sydney, a ride which was photographed and splashed all over the Australian newspapers.

In Auckland, he got a job as a platemaker for the *New Zealand Herald*, his original trade, but started building surfboards in his garage in Kohimarama. At first, he bought blanks from Peter Byers but he then built a mould in which to blow his own blanks. 'I really admire the pioneering work of Peter Byers in less than ideal conditions – there used to be twigs and all sorts of other rubble in Peter's early blanks.' Dave built his hinged moulds out of old metal pipe held together by fibreglass. He would mix the foam with an old food mixer. He made custom boards and 'pop-outs' but the pop-outs tended to bubble and delaminate after a short period of time so Dave abandoned that and went back to custom boards. All this was done in his garage with a large amount of noise and smell. 'You could never do that these days. There are too many laws against that sort of stuff in people's backyards – and quite right too.' He sold the boards from a small shop on the corner of Kohimarama Road and Tamaki Drive, and his wife sold board shorts there.

After living so close to the surf in Sydney, Dave felt quite isolated from the surf in Auckland City. Piha and the rest of the west coast seemed too far away and with family responsibilities added, he found that the surfing was put on hold. Dave spent time training for his surf life saving by paddling his ski on the harbour and swimming the beaches.

In the late 60s, Dave moved his board-making operation to Takapuna as that was the centre of the surf industry in Auckland City – an irony in Dave's mind considering the infrequency of surf at Takapuna. With the infamous Peter Way, he started Jackman Way Surfboards. At its peak, Jackman Way Surfboards

continued on page 59

Denis Quane

Denis is one of the stalwarts of surfing in New Zealand. He has been involved from the beginning of the surfboard revolution and still runs a surf and ski shop in Christchurch to this day. During the 1960s, he was a surfing oasis in a rather barren South Island, and was responsible for most of the board sales there.

Denis joined the Sumner Surf Life Saving Club, at the age of 11, and spent the 1950s riding surf skis and trying to perfect his surfing on longboards. While still at school, Denis began building his own surf skis and hollow paddleboards using skills he had picked up from Tony Johnson.

On leaving school Denis got a job as a trainee stock agent which was a bit of a privilege usually reserved for private school boys. He enjoyed being in the country but he had to spend too much time in an office so when the orders for longboards and surf skis began to stack up, he quit his job as a stock agent. This was quite a radical move in itself for those times but to be quitting a good career to build surfboards was hard for many to believe. Denis was lucky that he had supportive parents and a 'don't-give-a-damn' attitude. (Denis was contracted to remove the temporary sheds that were being used by the Sumner Surf Life Saving Club, and rather than dispose of them completely he rebuilt one in his own backyard as a place in which to build his surfboards – not strictly legal but good recycling.)

Denis was a keen competitor in the surf life saving carnivals and he travelled to New Plymouth, as a junior, for the 1959 national surf life saving champs. It was there that Denis saw the Malibu boards belonging to Rick Stoner and Bing Copeland. He was amazed by the new boards and returned to Christchurch determined to build foam and fibreglass surfboards.

Denis built his own mould and his business in Malibu boards soon took off. Three-quarters of the boards were sold in the North Island which was always the focus of Denis' attention. He felt that Quane Surfboards was the leader in surfboard

(left) **Denis on Sumner Beach, Christchurch, 1959. He is holding the first longboard he built, and in the background is the first surf ski he built.**

PHOTO DENIS QUANE

(above) **Denis Quane surfing a hollow longboard, Sumner Beach, Christchurch, 1962.**

(right) **Denis in the blank room of his Redcliffes factory, 1965.**

(right) **Cutback at Taylors Mistake, Christchurch, 1965.**

manufacturing right up until mid-60s. He didn't see anything coming from the North Island that threatened his position in those first years.

In order to keep up with technology and stay ahead of the other manufacturers in New Zealand, Denis used contacts in the USA and made regular trips to Sydney. His design influences also came from American and Australian magazines.

After Californian surf guru, Bob Cooper, spent some time shaping at Quane, Denis returned to California with him in 1966. He enjoyed great surfing at The Ranch and Rincon, and later in Mexico.

At home, Denis surfed mainly at Sumner and Taylors Mistake, plus later trips to Gore Bay and Magnet Bay. He competed in the national surfboard championships at New Plymouth, Gisborne and Christchurch. He still maintained surf life saving contacts but the time constraints of work meant no time to patrol. His club wouldn't let him go and defend his national titles. *'I remember being baled up in the street by the surf life saving seniors and blamed for the demise of surf life saving in New Zealand, and they called me a renegade and all sorts of stuff. It didn't bother me.'*

Denis was a ground-breaker for weekend trading after applying to open his surf shop for a few hours on Saturdays. Saturday trading was against the law in the 1960s so Denis had to get a lawyer and go to court to apply for a licence to open his shop. He was successful and Saturday trading was born in Christchurch in 1967. He was also amongst the first to sell surf clothing and to use a sales rep for his products.

Denis has remained active in the surf industry and in surf life saving, and is one of the true originals of New Zealand surfing. His skills in business and board building meant that his Christchurch factory was a leader in the industry when geographical isolation could have easily dissuaded someone less determined.

was turning out 20-30 boards per week. Fridays were always busy with surfers wanting their new boards to try out in the weekend. Dave: *'It didn't seem to matter that the board was still soft and needed 14 days to cure properly. They just wanted to get out there so off they went with their new board.'*

Dave says it was a love not money business making boards. It was always hard to get good materials and there was plenty of competition from Atlas Woods, Dunlop, Bob Davie and many others, including backyard board builders.

Dave Jackman was already a fully-fledged surf legend when he arrived in New Zealand but he made a significant contribution to the board building industry in New Zealand and inspired many local surfers along the way.

And the rest

It seems that just about all the early surfers had a go at building a board at some stage. The 'do it yourself' attitude was still strong in surfing and there were few people who could honestly be called 'experts' at board building. Also, the cost of a new board (up to £40) made it appealing for backyard shapers to try their hand. Smaller producers such as Kent, Heard, Wilson & Edwards, and Britwyn all built boards for local markets.

Peter Morse is an example of the backyard board builder, a breed that had discovered surfing, loved it and wanted cheap boards. In 1963, Pete started surfing on an Atlas Woods 9'3" at Milford Beach, aged 13. He and friend Greg Heap started making boards for themselves, and friends, under the PeterGreg label. They bought damaged blanks from Atlas Woods, the other supplies from the local hardware store, and started by copying their own Atlas Woods boards. The first attempts were a bit wobbly and heavy but things improved markedly by the time they had built about ten. There was a willing market for the cheaper boards amongst the local surfers.

PeterGreg produced about 40 surfboards. This provided the funds for a van and a surf trip around the South Island in 1965-66 when Peter was only 15 years old.

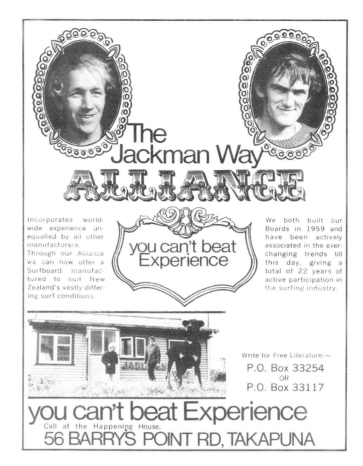

(left) Jackman Way was a partnership between two surfing legends, Dave Jackman and Peter Way. The business only survived a couple of years before both parties moved on – Dave back to surf life saving and Peter to New Plymouth. Dave Jackman: *'Peter spent a lot of time going surfing and hanging out with the potential customers – these days it would be called marketing. I spent my time at the factory filling the orders for the kids who wanted to emulate the Peter Way style.'*

At the end of 1966, Peter left school and went to Australia to go surfing. On his return in 1967, he got a job with Atlas Woods as a glasser and shaper. He was required to shape five boards per day, five days a week. He earned more than friends who were accountants, about $80-85 per week. This was a vast improvement on the backyard income of Peter Greg Surfboards and demonstrated a common career path for the board building pioneers.

As each of the new manufacturers got up and running, there was a big increase in the total number of people shaping, glassing, sanding, and performing all the other required tasks around a board shop. While they can't all be mentioned here, most were keen surfers of the day and included future performers such as Wayne Parkes, Alan Byrne, Steve King, Tony Ogilvy, Phil Jamisen and Rodney Dahlberg.

From First Wave to Second Wave, the originals carry on

Peter Byers

By 1963, Peter was a four-year veteran of board building and became the source of blanks for a number of the new entrants to the surfboard market. The materials were still hard to get and the demand for boards was steadily growing so Peter would purchase two drums of foam base and blow 35-40 blanks at a time.

By 1964-65, it became easier to get blanks from sources such as Atlas Woods, so Peter concentrated on his own board building. There was still a market for blanks, however, and Peter supplied Surfboards Gisborne when they set up in 1969.

Peter Byers Surfboards kept up with a steady demand for custom boards on the west coast. Peter still spent plenty of time in the water and sold many of his boards after showing what they could do in the waves – he seldom had a board of his own for long before someone would make an offer for it. Peter continued working from his factory in Piha until he finally closed up shop in the mid-70s.

Peter Miller

Peter continued to manufacture boards in Hamilton, mainly for surfers at Raglan and Mount Maunganui. He built and sold boards in his Inland Surf Shop, the first surf shop in Hamilton, up until 1965.

Peter entered the first (1963) nationals at Mount Maunganui and came second to Peter Way in the senior men, and third in the open men. He was a member of the Point Board Riders' Club and spent most of his time surfing at Raglan. Peter is believed to be the first surfer to have ridden Raglan, in 1960.

He closed the Inland Surf Shop in 1965 and moved to Lower Hutt, Wellington, for his fulltime job with Burroughs Business Machines. In Lower Hutt he opened the second Inland Surf Shop and sold Quane custom made boards.

Peter surfed overseas in Sydney and Hawaii, and moved to the United States in 1969. He is a true pioneer of New Zealand surfing, as surfer, board builder, explorer, competitor and retailer.

Denis Quane

By 1963-64, Denis had moved to a larger factory with up to eight employees. The business was running at such a pace that it was just a matter of trying to keep up with filling the orders and getting the boards away. 70-80% of the boards went to the North Island and were sold through outlets such as Dave Littlejohn's shop in New Plymouth, John Conway's shop in Wellington and Peter Miller's shop in Hamilton. Denis: *'I sold plenty of boards through various agents in Auckland, including Dave Jackman. In hindsight, I probably could have met the demand of all those centres but I didn't really have a clear overview at the time, concentrating purely on filling orders as fast as possible. I always looked to the north for business and it was only later in the 60s that I had agents in Dunedin, Timaru and Westport.'* Boards were also exported to Australia, Peru and the Channel Islands.

Denis' design influences were mainly from American and Australian magazines but he made regular trips to Sydney, and one to California, to keep up to date with the trends in board design. He had several overseas surfers working with him during the 1960s, including John McDermott (who had become a New Zealand citizen) and Bob Cooper from California.

In 1965, Denis secured a licence agreement with Barry Bennett in Australia which allowed him to use Bennett's accumulated expertise to mix and formulate foam for making blanks. He could now get a high level of control over the quality of the blanks allowing lighter and better boards.

Up until the late 60s, Quane Surfboards was pretty much the sole supplier of boards to surfers in the South Island but some other boards were available, such as Atlas Woods and Bob Davies. Alongside the boards, Denis produced clothing and a wetsuit branded with the Quane Surfboards logo. He also employed a sales rep to sell his products around the country.

(below) Peter Miller's first Inland Surf Shop, Hamilton, 1964. Boards were the main product in the early 60s before retailers realised the potential of surf clothing.

PHOTO PETER MILLER

What about the surfers?

It is estimated that there were 300 surfers in New Zealand in 1963, increasing to approximately 15-20,000 by 1968. It is easy to see where all the new surfboards were going.

The surfing boom had well and truly hit by the mid-60s. As shaping and technology improved, boards got shorter (from 10'-plus to approximately 9') and lighter, allowing younger surfers and females greater access to surfing. Popular breaks began to get crowded and loose boards began to fly, leading to further strife with the surf life saving movement.

Surfing changed quickly from a situation where most of the surfers knew each other and shared their knowledge, to a sport that was big business and full of learners (gremmies). What had been a 'black sheep' sport suddenly became a lot more mainstream (terms such as 'highway surfer' began to be coined for people who had a board on the car but never went surfing).

Whereas surfing in the late 50s to early 60s involved a relatively small number of individuals whose stories make up the early history of surfing, the mid- to late 60s were characterised by a huge increase in the number of people surfing. There were standouts in competition and daring deeds, and dramas both on and off the ocean, but most of the new recruits were happy to just buy a board, go to the beach and enjoy the pure thrill of surfing.

Meanwhile, at the beach ...

Lots of learner surfers descended on the beach during the mid-60s and, in those days before legropes, anybody who fell off left a 25-30 pound missile heading for the beach on the white water. This wasn't so much of a problem in the early 60s because of the small number of people surfing, the amount of room on the beaches and the skills of the existing surfers. However, as the popular beaches became more crowded with new surfers, swimmers began to get injured by the loose boards. This brought the surfers back into conflict with the surf life savers and local councils who felt responsible for keeping the beaches safe. Dave

Walpole has a folder full of correspondence and newspaper articles detailing the battles between the NZSRA and local councils over the rights of surfers at beaches.

'We will fight them on the beaches ...'

The problem was mainly confined to the city beaches of Auckland, Wellington and Christchurch but there was conflict at popular surf locations such as Waipu, Mount Maunganui, Gisborne, New Plymouth and Titahi Bay. Surf life savers were backed by local councils who saw the surfers as a renegade movement peopled by anti-establishment hooligans, and surf life savers as the socially sound keepers of the beach.

The worst conflicts appear to have occurred at Lyall Bay and Titahi Bay, in Wellington, Mount Maunganui's Main Beach and, ironically, Takapuna Beach in Auckland. Ironic because, at best, Takapuna enjoys occasional surf which can be good but small, and because the only surf life saving presence at the beach was a part-time club run by young women. However,

(above) **Mount Maunganui, 1966. As the popularity of surfing soared, loose boards meant danger for swimmers at the more popular beaches. Attempts to control surfers led to renewed conflict with surf life savers and local councils.**

PHOTO DAVE WALPOLE

61

Views of Mount Maunganui *(top)* **and Piha** *(bottom)* **indicate the huge number of surfers that had been attracted to the sport by the mid- to late 60s. None of the board riders had legropes and the loose boards caused administrative headaches for the surf life savers and real headaches for the swimmers.**

the beach is in the middle of New Zealand's largest city and, therefore, a large number of surfers called Takapuna home.

The local council found that they could not create surf lanes because the Auckland Water Safety Council had jurisdiction over the water at the beach. So, faced with no surf lanes and the prospect of surfers and swimmers colliding, the council chose to ban surfing, using an old bylaw, until the matter could be resolved in some other way. Wardens were appointed by the council to confiscate surfboards and fine errant surfers. (In April 1967, the East Coast Bays Borough Council banned surfing at all the East Coast Bays beaches except a 100-yard-wide surf lane at Rothesay Bay, which gets even less surf than Takapuna.)

Ross Gribble was the first and only surfer to be fined for surfing outside a surf lane, at Takapuna, on May 15 1968. The bylaw was challenged, and the Secretary for Marine, Mr O'Halloran, declared it illegal. He pointed out that the equivalent measures for a parking infringement would result in an owner's car being confiscated. Despite numerous efforts, the council was never able to legally enforce the ban on surfing at the beach mainly because they had no jurisdiction over the water (for the same reason they could not actually create surfing lanes in the water).

At Mount Maunganui, the surf life saving club at the main beach made sure that surfboards did not enter the flagged zones. A beach warden (Rex Cochrane) was appointed by the local council to patrol the rest of the larger Mount Maunganui beach

and ensure surfers were not endangering swimmers. Due to the large area and increasing number of surfers involved, the patrol was relatively impotent. There was again the legal dilemma of board confiscation and little if any was attempted. To top matters off, there was a certain lack of enthusiasm due to many of the surfers being ex-life savers, or relatives and friends of life savers, and a belief held by some in the surf life saving movement that the presence of the surfers was increasing the number of swimmers rescued. More often than not, however, the swimmers and surfers were interested in different parts of the beach and clashes were limited.

New Plymouth featured some rather more spirited clashes due to the presence of a very good surf break at Fitzroy Beach which was home to a very strong surf life saving club. There also appeared to be more antagonism at an individual level over members who had left surf life saving to go surfing.

Wayne Arthur: *'We used to have mighty arguments with the Fitzroy Surf Life Saving Club. They didn't want us to surf at the beach and used to set traps for us. Even on rainy, bleak days with no self-respecting swimmer in sight, they would come down blowing whistles and try to clear the water. The cops got involved and it became a real battle of wits. Two surfers took to the club's watch tower with a paint brush. It made the front page of the local rag and put us all off-side with the population for a good decade.'*

In the greater Taranaki area there were some minor show-downs at Oakura and Opunake, where surf life saving clubs were present but, in general, the large area of surfable coastline and small number of surfers meant that the two factions could get about their business without too many disputes.

Wellington's Lyall Bay and Titahi Bay, just north of Welling-ton, were the centres of some quite bitter squabbling between surfers, surf life savers and local councils.

The beaches in question were very popular swimming beaches, had good surf and were close to a large population base. (A 1967 newspaper article on summer-time crowding at Titahi Bay reported 57 surfers in the water.) In summer, boards and swimmers were colliding. Surfers were also being blamed for bottles, broken glass and other litter being left at the beaches.

The National Water Safety Committee was moving to zone the beaches without consulting the surfers so the Wellington Surfing Club (WSC) was established in 1965 in order to legitimise the sport and get some input into zoning discussions.

Both surfers, represented by WSC founder and president Peter Fitzsimmons, and surf life savers agreed that something needed to be done. The severity of the measures was the area of dispute. Peter Fitzsimmons argued that board riders were performing a large number of unrecorded rescues, generally surfed in areas away from the swimmers and used the beaches throughout the year, unlike the swimmers. The councils and surf life savers were aiming for compulsory registration numbers for surfboards (so loose boards could be traced back to owners for unspecified punishment) and permanent zoning of the beaches to keep surfers away from swimmers. Peter put the case for zoning in summer only and that there must be consideration of where the best surf was found on the beaches – there was no point in having a surfing zone where there were poor waves. The WSC encouraged all its members to register their boards with the club in order to preempt a council move for compulsory board registration for which they would also charge a sizeable fee.

A registration day was held in April 1966 but it brought out the rebellious best in the surfers and only 40 of the 80 WSC members turned up to register their boards. However, it did buy some time. Further PR moves by Peter Fitzsimmons (such as instigating surf rescue, resuscitation and 440-yard swim tests as prerequisites for joining the club) helped keep the establishment at bay long enough for the problem to drift into the early 1970s and the arrival of the legrope. Legropes suddenly meant that all those surfboards were now tied to their owners, and the major source of antagonism between surfers and surf life savers virtually disappeared.

Chris Ransley joined Gisborne's Midway Surf Life Saving Club late in the 1960s after an approach from Jack Griffin, the president of Midway. *'Jack recognised the potential of the surfers*

not only for on-the-spot surf rescue but also as competitors for surf life saving. Glen Sutton, Benny Hutchings and I were national title holders for team competition in the early 1970s. There was not too much animosity between surf life saving and surfing in Gisborne. I found it perfectly easy to do the patrol work and go surfing. It tended to be individuals who made it difficult. There was some beach zoning before legropes but it was sensible and the surfers got the areas they wanted. It didn't last long and wasn't well policed.'

Bob Comer: *'The surf life savers saw surfers as a social threat too because we were more attractive to the women. We had the cars, and we had better music and better parties. The culture was attractive because it was new and alternative.'*

Wherever surf life saving clubs were situated around the country, there was some degree of resentment over the defection of beach-going youths to surfing and the encroachment of boards and surfers into swimming areas. However, in most cases, the two got on with their respective pursuits without major conflict and often sharing the same personnel.

To go where no other has ...

An obvious way to get away from the problem of crowds and surf life savers was to go on 'surfari'. Trips lasting whole days, weekends and even weeks was one of the things that brought surfers into conflict with old friends, families, girlfriends/boyfriends and

(above) **Victoria University Surf Riders Club outing to Castlepoint on the Wairarapa coast, 1967. Mike McGlynn was one of the founders of the VUSRC:** *'We had a grant from the Student Council to buy a big tent and to hire a bus for occasional trips away. The trips were well attended and any left over money went on kegs of beer. Castlepoint was popular because it could turn on good surf and because it boasted a fantastic pub. At "closing time" the curtains would be drawn, the piano player and guitarists fuelled up and numerous trays of crayfish would be handed around. The party would go on into the night with an interesting blend of surfers, farmers, fishermen, shearers and sundry others.'*

(above) **Mike McGlynn, Lyall Bay, 1967.**

(left) **Mike McGlynn** (centre) **and friends, Mount Maunganui, summer of 1966-67.** *'The summer trip was always popular. This is a group of the Paekakariki and Lower Hutt surfers. We didn't get much surf but we partied hard. As you can see, there still wasn't much in the way of label surf clothing around.'*

PHOTO DAVE REES-GEORGE

(right) Adrian Rogers surfing Goat Island Bay, Northland, 1965. A story about this trip appeared in *New Zealand Surf Magazine* describing it as the first time Goat Island Bay had been surfed.

(below) Mike Gardiner *(far right)* and friends carefully considering the surf and the rocks before going out, Opunake, 1964.

PHOTO MIKE GARDINER

PHOTO MIKE GARDINER

When Mike Gardiner went to Opunake in 1963, he found abundant surf and no one in the water. With big waves and rocky breaks, however, a degree of caution was required and any friends who came down to join him in the surf were welcomed.
(above) 'Some guy called "Pommy" on a big day', 1964.
(right, l to r) Peter Ray, Mike Gardiner, Dave Littlejohn and Randy Butler, Opunake, 1964.

PHOTO MIKE GARDINER

employers. No other sport so completely captivated its participants and that was something non-surfers found hard to understand.

Taff Kennings was a Takapuna local who covered hundreds of miles in search of waves, spending most weekends on the road and only just getting back in time for work on Mondays. *'With a bit of work you could get a long way on a surf trip. For example, a trip to Piha from Takapuna cost about 50 cents each if you had a car load of surfers.'*

Once a local beach had been surfed, understood and appreciated, the urge to explore farther afield began to manifest itself. Also, the arrival of overseas magazines and movies made surfers aware of the different types of breaks being surfed and inspired a new wave of travel in search of the best point and reef breaks.

While in the early 60s, just about every surf trip discovered a previously unridden break, the mid-60s represented a time when a large proportion of the coastline had been explored but was still relatively free of surfers. The main 'surf centres', for example Mount Maunganui, Piha and Lyall Bay, were becoming crowded when the surf was good and that provided another incentive to go exploring.

Huge distances were covered in huge cars in the hopes of finding good, empty surf. New areas were still being opened up such as Goat Island, north of Auckland, and Great Barrier Island.

Mike Gardiner epitomised the spirit of discovery in the early 60s. Mike was studying pharmacy and after a less than sparkling first year, he went to explore the surf potential in Opunake. *'I got lucky and landed a job as an assistant to the local pharmacist with time off when the surf was good. I discovered most of the nearby reef breaks during my six months there (1963-64). There were a few surfers around Opunake at the time but they stuck to the beach leaving me to discover the points and reefs. I started sending news to my friends about the surf potential at Opunake and soon the visitors began to arrive.'*

Back in Auckland, Mike found a group of surfer/divers who were keen to explore Great Barrier Island. *'We were the first surfers to go there and proved quite a novelty for the locals. We lived*

continued on page 68

Del Surfboards

Dave Littlejohn

Dave started surfing on a board he had built himself in the summer of 1956-57. He continued to surf the same board until the arrival of Frank Wilkin and Quane boards inspired him to open the New Plymouth Surf Shop in 1962.

Dave was a mentor to all the early surfers in the Taranaki area, selling them the boards and equipment they needed, and taking car-loads of young surfers on many voyages of exploration around the uncharted surf coast. He took photos of the local surfers and breaks, and played surf movies in hired halls which provided a raucous night out for surfers and non-surfers alike.

Dave set up Del Surfboards together with Nigel Dwyer who had travelled to New Plymouth for the 1965 nationals. *'I provided the finance and Nige supplied the technical skills. Nigel and the boys built them, and I packed, sold and delivered them. We were making up to 40 boards per week and I was delivering 40 or 50 boards per month over to Gisborne which were sold through John Penny's Sports Store. We also supplied Ken Griffin in Napier. I would load up the Galaxy and a board trailer and roar off across the island.'*

Dave started out as a surf life saver but surfing took over his life and then the business almost took over his surfing. *'I concentrated on running the business and left the rowdy stuff up to Nige and the boys. I got the supplies in and put them all on piece work rates because they spent so much time in the surf. They would surf all day and work all night. The noise at night from that house would drive the neighbours crazy. Trevor Pollard was our best shaper because he didn't surf and would actually get some work done.'*

As a founding member of the New Plymouth Board Riders, Dave showed his skills on the administrative side of the sport and, although he was not a competitor, Dave was involved in organising most of the contests that took place in the Taranaki area.

Dave eventually sold his share of Del to Nigel in 1973-74 and moved on to a rather more peaceful life having acted as mentor to a whole generation of young surfers in New Plymouth.

PHOTO DAVE LITTLEJOHN

(above) The New Plymouth Surf Shop, 1963. Dave's Ford Galaxy is parked out front with a good load of boards on top. Dave joined forces with Nigel Dwyer in 1965 to create Del Surfboards.

Supplied by :
NEW PLYMOUTH
Surf Shop
144 Courtenay St.
Phone 83964

**(right) Dave surfing at a favourite surf spot he discovered – Waiwhakaiho, New Plymouth, 1963.
Peter Way: 'I used to call Dave Littlejohn the "Green Keeper" because he always used to sit out on the shoulder, away from the impact zone. And the first time I met Nigel Dwyer he immediately started shaping up to me and we had a big scrap – we've been thick as thieves ever since.'**

PHOTO DAVE LITTLEJOHN

Nigel Dwyer

Nigel started surfing in 1958-59 at Cronulla, Australia. He worked in surfboard factories with Brian Jackson and Norm Casey, and became a skilled glasser. Terry Tumeth's reports of good surf and cheap icecream in New Zealand were enough to convince Nigel it was worthy of a visit.

He arrived in Gisborne, with a group of fellow Cronulla surfers, looking for Bob Davie, their only contact in New Zealand. Nigel swears that Bob hid for a week when he heard they were in town. Their first view of Gisborne was the deserted main street on Saturday morning. They found accommodation at the YMCA and were only supposed to spend one night but ended up staying for a month because the owners were too afraid to throw them out.

Nigel bought a 1938 Packard which was big enough to take the whole team and their equipment. They nailed on roof racks, luggage rack and fruit boxes inside to take all the gear, and then roped everything down. They also lashed a motorbike to one mudguard and a bicycle to the other. It made for an imposing surfwagon.

Nigel remembers Gisborne as a wonderful time in his life but freely admits that he and his fellow Australians drove the town mad. It was a good time to leave when he headed over to New Plymouth for the 1965 nationals.

(above) **Nigel judging a contest on a cold and windy day in New Plymouth, 1967.**

(above) **Blanks stacked against the walls inside the house that acted as the Del factory. (l to r) Nigel Dwyer, Trevor Pollard, Roger 'Hobbs' Gordon, Graeme 'Scruffy' Dunne.**

At the nationals, Nigel met Dave Littlejohn who owned a shop in town that sold surfboards. He approached Nigel about making boards in New Plymouth. Nigel agreed but decided to first go home to Australia and get some advice from his ex-employer, Norm Casey.

In Wellington, after first fortifying himself with beer, Nigel stowed away on a cruise ship bound for Brisbane. He managed not to get caught at the dock in Brisbane and returned to Sydney. He learnt how to make moulds and blow blanks from Norm Casey and then came back to New Plymouth to set up.

The name Del was the result of abbreviating the names

Dwyer & Littlejohn. As soon as the new moulds and templates had been made, Del Surfboards began producing boards in an old house in New Plymouth and selling them through Dave Littlejohn's shop.

Nigel served as president of the Cape Board Riders Club (later New Plymouth Board Riders Club) for a number of years. He created the Del International Trophy and, in the 70s, the Del Invitational which brought together all the 'top' surfers in New Zealand for a weekend of non-competitive surfing in Taranaki – an 'expression session'. And, of course, there was a big party on the Saturday night.

A lot of Nigel's contribution to surfing in New Zealand occurred from 1970 onwards and is, therefore, outside the scope of this book. However, even between 1965 and 1970, he had such an influence that he is mentioned by most of his peers as an essential ingredient in the 60s mix.

The real charm of Nigel does not appear in a list of his achievements for Del Surfboards or New Zealand surfing, it is apparent when talking to other surfers and hearing the numerous stories of what a rogue he is. Nigel has had a significant influence on surfing in Taranaki and the country as a whole but he has brought real character to the sport in a way that would either get him a laugh or get him arrested.

(left) **Nigel checking the lines on a very groovy looking 'Tracker' board from Del, 1967.**

(far left, l to r) **Nigel Dwyer, Robbie Walsh, Merv Moses, 1969. Nigel:** *'The arrival of wetsuits in Taranaki was fantastic. A shipment would arrive and customers would be waiting at the door to snatch up whatever they could get.'*

(above and right) In the summer of 1964-65, Mike Gardiner organised a trip to Great Barrier Island to surf and dive. He was rewarded with ample pickings, in all forms, from the ocean.
(right, l to r) Mike Gardiner and Dennis Markson, a surfer/diver from Maroubra in Australia.

(right) One of Mike's companions to Great Barrier Island was Phil 'Turkey' Delaney. 'They called me "Turkey" because I could catch the turkeys that were prevalent around Karekare, where I grew up. But it really stuck after a turkey hunt we organised out of North Piha Surf Life Saving Club. We had caught some turkeys and were on our way back to North Piha for a roast up when the car ran out of petrol at the top of the Piha hill. We walked all the way back to the surf club and started plucking. Next thing we knew, the irate farmer who owned the turkeys walks in and all hell breaks loose. He had followed the trail of feathers to the club. He eventually settled down and said he would not report us to the police if we made a £50 donation to the SPCA. That was a hell of a lot of money in those days but we eventually raised it. Peter Way went into the SPCA office in the city and the clerk just about dropped off his chair when he told him how much he wished to donate – they made Peter a life member!'

there for about eight months, surviving on fresh fish and crayfish, and surfing.'

Going on 'surfari' is a vital part of being a surfer and every participant in the sport can probably relate at least one tale of a wild surf trip into the unknown. There are hundreds of sordid tales that could go with the memoirs recorded in this book, some of which can be found alongside the photographs herein, but the following gives an idea of the scale of some of the surf missions.

Tim Murdoch: 'We picked up Bob Davie at Mount Maunganui and drove to Te Awanga, Napier, where we got some good surf. Then we drove over to New Plymouth which was not so good so we decided to go to Kaikoura where we had two excellent days at Maungamanu. We then went on to Christchurch to see Denis Quane but the surf never really got good there so headed back to Lyall Bay. The waves were good there. We drove back to Raglan, which was average, but we heard that Piha was good so we drove straight back there and found the bar was working perfectly with nobody out. Unfortunately, I dislocated my shoulder and had to get the others to drive me to Auckland Hospital over the bumpy Piha road. Bob just wanted to get back to the Mount but realised he had left all his stuff out at Piha. That was a good, bad and indifferent trip.'

In the words of Peter Way: 'Chris Prentice, who was a non-drinker, would drive after a Friday night binge and the crew could wake up in the car on Saturday anywhere between New Plymouth, Gisborne, Whangamata and Ninety Mile Beach.'

And the weather today ...

Another reason for the enormous distances covered in search of surf was the absence of reliable weather information. Guess work and a good phone network of people who lived near the surf were the best sources of information. It was still very hard to predict what the conditions would be like by the time one arrived at the surf and many a trip ended in disappointment.

Peter Fitzsimmons: 'One problem that confronted all the surfers in the 1960s was the lack of accurate weather information. The Post Office used to have reports from the manned lighthouses and these

(l to r) Martin Hall and Rick Bradley helping Campbell Ross negotiate the Model A up a tricky ramp at Tokerau Beach, Northland, 1965.

PHOTO: BOB COMER

would provide some clues as to where the best surf might be found. But the most valuable sources of information were local farmers and residents at key surf spots. An effort was made to develop a rapport with these people and educate them as to how to read the surf. From there, a quick phone call could save many hours of travel.'

Discovering the lost tribes

All the travelling by local surfers, and the presence of overseas surfers touring the country, meant that surfers living in the more remote areas of New Zealand, who had previously been blissfully unaware of crowds in any form – swimmers, surfers or surf life savers – were suddenly being brought up to date with the rest of the surfing world. In the Far North, Bob and Joan Atherton were joined by Neville Masters to make a total of three dedicated surfers for the huge area of coastline that the Far North represented. Bob Atherton: 'In the mid-60s, we could still drive to all our favourite spots with little fear of seeing other surfers. It could get crowded though; I still have fantastic memories of a surf at Great Exhibition Bay with 40-50 dolphins. However, after the appearance of Shipwreck Bay in The Endless Summer, the number of visitors to the Far North increased dramatically. When conditions were right, we could wake up in the morning to find twenty people asleep in the lounge, having arrived in the early hours of the morning after

(below) Camp site at Taupo Bay during the same trip, Northland, 1965.
(below right) Another view of Taupo Bay, in 1963, with regular visitors, (l to r) Pat Brennan, Joan Atherton (lying down), Bob Atherton, Jeremy Busck and Neville Masters.

(above) Paradise Bay, Northland, 1964. (l to r) Doug Lamb and unknown.

(right) Shipwreck Bay, Northland, 1965. (l to r) Bob Atherton and Neville Masters. Ken Clark: 'I was a keen explorer in Northland, together with Bob and Joan Atherton, Doug Lamb and Ross Edmonson. We may have been the first to surf Shipwreck Bay, at the bottom of Ninety Mile Beach. I wasn't actually able to surf that day due to a knee injury from surfing the previous day. Doug Lamb took the first wave and fell off when he hit the submerged boiler of the wreck in the middle of the bay. We couldn't believe how long the rides were.'

(far right) Volkswagens belonging to the Athertons, Neville Masters and Ken Clark pulled over for a check of Shipwreck Bay from opposite the old Panorama Tea Rooms. Photo is looking north up Ninety Mile Beach.

(left) Bob Atherton slides along another Shipwreck Bay face, Northland, 1964.
Joan Atherton: *'I can still vividly recall a period in the late 60s when Shipwreck Bay broke at chest high or bigger for 15 weeks in a row. It was summer and we would rush home from work for a quick dinner and then get out for a surf before it got dark.'*

(right) Christine poses against Roger Land's trusty Vauxhall while on a 1962 'surfari' to Whangamata.

(below, l to r) Brett Knight, Phil Cooney and Mike Cooney on Bailey's Beach, Dargaville, 1965.
Tui Wordley: *'We would take this Austin A55 anywhere ... it was better than a 4-wheel drive.'*

a long drive from Auckland.' Neville Masters: *'We would just get the map out and see which roads actually went right down to the beach. We always had the surf to ourselves so Bob, Joan and I probably discovered most of the Far North spots. People would stop to watch us surf because it was still so unknown.'*

The closer one moved to the main cities, the more in touch local surfers were. In Whangarei, Tui Wordley had regular contact with the surfers of the Far North and Auckland: *'In the beginning (the first 9 months or so), there were only the Edge boys (Ross and Don) and myself. Then the clubbies at Waipu became involved, and visitors from Auckland and overseas started arriving. We surfed locally most of the time but we travelled as far afield as Ahipara (Shipwreck Bay) in the north, and New Plymouth and Gisborne in the south.*

'Whangarei had a surf club to which I belonged, Tatahi Surfriders, and I was a Foundation Member, Club Captain and Committee member. I competed in our club competitions and also the first nationals at the Mount in 1963 – I placed fourth in the final behind 'Hermit' McDermott, Peter Way and Peter Miller. I still think of it as a fun thing and don't take it too seriously – trophies lose their shine and only collect dust after a while.

'I still have fond memories of Friday nights in "downtown" Whangarei, meeting at "Surfies Corner" (Walton St and Rathbone St) to find out where the parties were for the weekend, who was going surfing and where, and other general happenings. On the other corner was the rugby and surf life saving mob, and across the street were the motor cycle boys. Having an interest in all three areas, I would do the rounds of them all.

'Big parties, stirs, rages or whatever you call them were a big part of the whole scene. Tatahi Surfriders had a reputation for good parties and it got to the stage where the parties became invitation only affairs. Also, Tim Murdoch used to send me surf movies like Big Wednesday (the original) *and* Slippery When Wet *and I would show them for the locals.'*

Further south, in Napier, Ken Griffin and his fellow surfers relished visits from touring surfers as a source of new equipment and information. *'By 1963, there were around 30 dedicated riders*

(left) Dave Walpole and friends head out for a surf at Spot X (Waiwhakaiho), New Plymouth, 1964.
PHOTO DAVE WALPOLE

(below) Unknown surfers sharing the perfect looking peaks of East End Beach, New Plymouth, 1968.
PHOTO NEIL REID

(above, l to r) Ken Griffin and Garry Fraser, Arapaoanui Beach, Hawkes Bay, 1965. 'The best waves were at Westshore Reef and Hardinge Road – good shape and easy to ride. Waipatiki was the most consistent beach break and Stingray Bay offered a good right hand reef break. Only the keen surfers went to Stingray Bay as it was a half-hour walk around the rocks or a long paddle. Te Awanga is a good right hander but needs a big swell in the Bay before it works.'

(above) Surfers gathered for a contest between Valley Surf Riders Club and Christchurch Breakwater Club, Kaikoura 1967/68. Check out the snow! Wetsuits were still uncommon around this time so it was a hardy person who went surfing in these temperatures.

(right) Maungamanu, Kaikoura, 1965. South Islanders enjoyed empty waves long after the popular North Island breaks began to get crowded, and there were plenty of top quality waves like this point break.

in Hawkes Bay and if there were eight or ten riders at one spot, we thought it was crowded. We rode all year around with no wetsuits, only football jerseys to keep warm. Around 1965, board riding really boomed with quite a few schoolboys taking up surfing. Two of the best were Ian Davidson and Brian Wilson.

'Bob Davie called into Napier and stayed with me a few times in the late 60s. He showed us the latest boards and how to ride them. One board was only 5'8" which was very radical for that time. Bob's best board was "The Instrument" – about 7'6" long, buoyant and easy to paddle, turn and ride. That board was very popular in Napier.'

Despite the close proximity of Quane Surfboards in Christchurch, Dunedin was a long way behind the rest of the country in terms of surfing. After Bart Smaill's first attempts at board building in 1959-60 (inspired by the boards of Rick Stoner and Bing Copeland), it took a further two to three years to get a group of about 10 surfers established in Dunedin. 'We surfed Saint Clair mainly because there seemed little point in driving around looking for surf when it was right there on our front doorstep. Saint Clair on a good day is as good as anywhere else I have surfed.'

With little need to travel for surf and few visitors arriving, Dunedin lived in its own surf world until about 1963 when the main board builders from the north (Quane, Atlas Woods, Dunlop) started selling their boards in town.

Neil Reid: 'The first boards I remember seeing were brought from Australia by Graeme Nisbett and Cyril Cousins. They were

8-9' and 10', respectively, fibreglass over balsa. I bought my first foam/fibreglass board from John Wilson, an Atlas Woods pop-out which was brittle and easily dinged. Boards from Atlas Woods, Quane and Dunlop were starting to appear in the shops by the mid-1960s. Denis Quane was the best source of boards but it wasn't until 1963-64 that his boards were readily available.'

Between surf club patrols and setting shark nets off Saint Clair, Neil, Trevor Clark, Les Jordan, Grant (Nuts) Nisbett, Johnny and Cyril Cousins and Ian Maskill explored as far and wide as possible for surf around the Dunedin coast. (Les Jordan was killed by a shark in 1964 and shark attacks were a constant thought for the surfers thereafter.) Wherever they went, they were usually the first to surf a break – Murderers Beach, Kaka Point and just about every break between Oamaru and the Chaslands.

Neil Reid: 'There were just a few of us surfing anyway and we were all still surf life saving club members, even if we were spending more and more time surfing. The surf clubs were still the only places with hot showers, an important consideration in the cold water of Dunedin. During surf life saving carnivals in the early 1960s, the surf club would close off the Esplanade and set up floodlights for night surfing – boards, canoes, boats and any other craft that could be found.

'I made the trip to New Plymouth for the nationals in 1965. It was pretty wild – I still remember Paul von Zalinski "car surfing" down the main street of New Plymouth. I never went to any other competitions, however, as it was too expensive to travel from Dunedin.'

The pattern was repeated in most of the small coastal towns of New Zealand. The first surfers would arrive, spreading the 'gospel', then local converts would scour the countryside for boards and make attempts at building their own until the arrival of Atlas Woods, Quane and Dunlop boards in approximately 1963. Surfers who made the effort to explore the surf potential of these distant locations would be greeted with open arms as sources of new information and equipment. There was little if any strife from crowding or splitting from surf life saving, most of the surfers in distant locations being surf life savers as well.

(inset, l to r) Neil Reid and an unknown surfer at Saint Clair, Dunedin, April 1964. *'We were using our life saving paddle boards and getting the hang of going along the face of the waves.'*

(above, l to r) Neil Reid and Cyril Cousins. Neil Reid: *'This is how I remember Saint Clair – summer time, perfect right handers, lined up to the horizon, and just me and a few friends out.'*

(right) Neil Reid: *'This was a common occurrence – my life saving team waiting on the beach for me to come in so they could get on with the competition. Luckily for me, they tolerated my surfing and I could still do both sports.'*

THREE PHOTOS NEIL REID

PHOTO NEIL REID

PHOTO ROGER LAND

(above) Neil Reid at Saint Clair, Dunedin, 1966. *'We had just discovered wetsuits which was an incredible improvement for surfers in Dunedin. You can imagine what a winter surf in Dunedin was like without one.'*
(right) Roger Land sent this photo of a Dunedin 'original' to Alan Godfery in 1963.

(right, l to r) Paul Griffin, John Joyce, George Peabody and Jim Mowtell pictured with Miss Hawaii International and her attendants, Hawaii, 1963.

PHOTO JIM MOWTELL, CHAS LAKE COLLECTION

Falling off the edge of the earth

While local exploration was in full swing by the mid-60s, international travel began to find favour as well. New Zealanders were hosting increasing numbers of surfers from overseas and curiosity began to emerge over what surf was available in other countries.

Tim Murdoch was probably our pioneer of foreign surfing, being a regular traveller to Hawaii, California and Queensland from 1960 onwards. Campbell Ross was in Australia by 1963 where he made the finals of the Bells Beach International.

By the mid-60s, going on a surf trip to Australia was becoming more common and was deemed to be essential for anybody with thoughts of competitive surfing. Sydney and the Gold Coast were the most common destinations but, as usual, New Zealanders could be found in every corner of Australia where there was surf. In the spirit of trans-Tasman frugality amongst surfers, stowing away on the cruise ships bound for Australia became a regular event. Taff Kennings: *'Each year Peter Way, Steve King and I would travel to Australia on board the Oriental Queen to go surfing. It cost about £40 and was the cheapest way to get to Australia. Well, not quite the cheapest ... stowing away was a common occurrence amongst the young surfers and they would take turns at sleeping in the cabin and eating in the restaurant. Coat pockets would be filled with food to share out. Steve King took the prize for cheek, introducing himself to the captain and dining at his table while he was a stowaway. Gavin Redfern was caught one year and had to work his fare for the rest of the trip — he eventually became a purser on the ship.'*

Gail Patty went to Australia for a winter in the late 60s. She and a car load of women friends followed a favourite pattern for visiting New Zealanders: *'We bought a big black Al Capone car, 5 boards on top, and surfed from Sydney to Noosa. We slept on the beach and when we were broke we survived on sugar cane and bananas from the fields.'*

Pilgrimages were also made to Hawaii by New Zealand surfers but the extra cost meant it was visited less often.

continued on page 79

Mr President
Dave Walpole

Dave was the co-creator and first president of the New Zealand Surf Riders' Association (NZSRA) in 1963. He grew up in Wellington but in the summer of 1953-54, he went to Mount Maunganui on holiday and saw his first surfers – Jock Carson and friends on longboards. He met Dave Murdoch on the beach and Dave allowed him to have a go on his longboard. The instructions he received for catching a wave were, *'Paddle like hell then stand up!'*

Dave Walpole moved to Tauranga in 1956, joining both the army and the Mount Maunganui Surf Life Saving Club. He spent most of his time on a 'teardrop' surf ski until Garth Tapper took pity on him and lent Dave a longboard. He rode the longboard until about 1960 when the new Malibu boards started arriving.

Dave is another who attended the 1959 surf life saving nationals at Oakura and remembers seeing Rick Stoner and Bing Copeland with their Malibu boards. Dave's first Malibu board was a 'Made by Mo' (Jim Mowtell) that had made it to the Mount. *"There weren't too many of us surfing in those early days but I had some great days with Tony Crosby, Barry Magee, Rex Cochrane, Richard Carr and Ces Marsh, and Campbell Ross was probably one of the first to visit our beach."*

Dave was president of the NZSRA from 1963 to 1966 before he went to Malaya with the army. During his time as president he fought hard to stop beach zoning and board registration schemes, accumulating folders full of correspondence and newspaper clippings. He tried to get surfers to join the clubs in order to counter the negative image that the public had of surfers. He was not competitive himself but enjoyed getting everyone together for the competitions.

Dave spent more time socialising with the surf life savers than the surfers, still lamenting that the two could not be under one association. He would attend the surf life saving carnivals

PHOTO GEOFF LOGAN, PHOTO NEWS

(left) Dave carrying out his duties as president of the NZSRA. Here he is presenting John Bonas with a prize during a Gisborne Board Riders club contest.

PHOTO DAVE WALPOLE

(above) Dave enjoying the solitude of surfing during a storm at Mount Maunganui in 1963.

(right) Dave Walpole executes a cutback of some panache at Mount Maunganui, 1964.

PHOTO DAVE WALPOLE

(above) **Dave Walpole, with his son Garth, enjoying an endless summer at Mount Maunganui, 1964.**

then head straight off for a surf.

In the course of his travels with the army, Dave was lucky enough to camp at the rifle range in New Plymouth, directly in front of what was then known as Spot X (Waiwhakaiho). He fondly recalls many surf sessions there with no one else out. He is also confident that he was the first to surf Waitotara, north of Wanganui, which he says is a fantastic right hander when conditions are right.

Dave returned to New Zealand, from Malaya, in 1968 and found the surf scene to be very different with larger crowds, more aggression and short boards. He was stationed at Papakura so he took up surf life saving and surfing at Piha and Muriwai. He gave up surfing in the early 1970s, due to injuries, but today is still an active and respected surf life saver at Port Waikato.

(above) **Peter Fitzsimmons presents Gail Patty with her trophy for winning the women's section of the 1967 nationals, held at Gisborne.**

Peter Fitzsimmons

Peter has been involved with surfing for 40 years, as surfer, administrator and retailer. From the mid-60s to early 70s, Peter was the official voice of the NZSRA, getting into several pro-longed 'scraps' with borough councils and surf life saving clubs over attempted restrictions on surfing.

Surfing for Peter began in 1959 at Lyall Bay, Wellington, while he was still a member of the Lyall Bay Surf Life Saving Club. When surfing came along and completely consumed the time of some of the younger members, it was frowned upon by the senior members of the club. However, the surfing bug had taken hold of Peter and there was a lot of coastline to explore.

Peter owned and ran a surf shop in Wellington, The Corner Surf Shop, from 1965-1975. He helped start the Wellington Surfing Club in 1965 and attended his first nationals in 1965 at New Plymouth. Peter joined the NZSRA as chief instructor (an educational role) before becoming president when Dave Walpole resigned in 1966.

Peter was a tireless worker for the NZSRA and spent a lot of time and effort on trying to avoid conflicts with councils and public bodies who wanted to control and restrict surfing. He presented a reasonable and well-spoken front for what was still considered a rather anti-establishment sport. It was a difficult job as a lot of the surfing community were happy to be outsiders and in conflict with the rest of society.

Peter continued as president of NZSRA until 1972 but felt surfing lost its purity in the 70s and he tended back towards surf life saving in the 70s and 80s. These days he is still involved in the administration of both sports and spends plenty of time in the water.

Jim Mowtell, Paul Griffin and John Joyce went to Hawaii in 1963 and were some of the first New Zealanders to go surfing there. When John Paine finished university in November 1964, he headed straight for Hawaii. *'I met up with Jim Mowtell, John Joyce and Paul Griffin, and surfed all the famous locations I could. I still vividly remember one special day at Honolua Bay – it was just one of those magical days. The waves were perfect and it was just me and Fred van Dyke out surfing. One to remember.'*

It's not about winning or losing ...

Travelling overseas to get experience in competitive surfing was a far cry from the more humble beginnings of the nationals. From the first national surfing competition in 1963, at Mount Maunganui, through to the 1966 nationals at Gisborne, competitive surfing enjoyed its heyday in New Zealand. Through these years, the competitions still enjoyed the original spirit of surfers getting together to have fun, swap news and ideas, and have a big party. Friends would surf one heat then judge the next, providing the equivalent of the present-day 'peer review'. It was a successful recipe that inspired local surf clubs to begin having interclub competitions outside of the nationals.

The first regional surf club, North Reef Board Club, was established in 1962 at Takapuna (that place again!) in Auckland. Point Board Riders followed soon after, in 1963, and Mount Maunganui Board Riders formed at the same time as the first nationals in 1963. From there, clubs established themselves rapidly over the next few years to a point where 28 clubs were represented at the 1967 nationals (in fact, by 1966 surfers had to be members of a regional surf club in order to be eligible).

The first two national competitions boasted some reasonable prizes (for example, a surfboard donated by Atlas Woods) and limited fame but the focus was mainly on getting the few surfers in the country together for a fun time.

Once the New Zealand Surf Riders' Association was formed

PHOTO DAVE WALPOLE

(above) A heat of an inter-club contest between Mount Board Riders and Gisborne Board Riders, held at 'Stockroute', Gisborne, 1965.

(left) Two of the club magazines that were produced during the heyday of local surf clubs.

(right) Complete with emblazoned jackets, New Zealand sent this team to compete for the 'Tasman Bucket' trophy in Australia, 1968. The contest was won by the New South Wales team but New Zealand came a creditable third. The 'Tasman Bucket' event was meant to provide New Zealand's surfers with more international experience but the contest only lasted one year because the Australians lost interest in it. (l to r) Taff Kennings, Wayne Parkes, Peter Fitzsimmons (Team Manager), Alan Byrne, Doug Hislop, Bob Davie.

(below, l to r) Taff Kennings, Wayne Parkes and Rod Allison. These three surfers from Takapuna were competing in the junior section of the 1964 nationals held at Mount Maunganui.

in 1963, contact with the international surf bodies began. Thus, the possibility arose for the best surfers in the country to be New Zealand's representatives at international surf contests. This was extremely exciting for the youngsters who were involved in the sport, being from a country where international travel was still rare and expensive. Wayne Parkes: *'I wanted to win the nationals so I could get the overseas trips. It was the only way I would get to places like that at sixteen and seventeen.'*

The first New Zealand representative surfing team left for San Diego and the World Surfing Championships in 1966. The team consisted of the new senior men's champion, Wayne Parkes (17 years old), the junior champion, Alan Byrne (15 years old), and the surfer considered to be the next best in the country, Rodney Fawcett of Christchurch (15 years old). Dave Burns, from Gisborne, also went with the team as New Zealand's top judge, and chaperone. Alan managed a fifth placing in the five-mile paddleboard race but no other significant results were posted by the New Zealanders in this competition which was won by Nat Young.

Around the same time as the idea of sending our surfers to international competitions was being proposed, the sport was

going through a big growth spurt and new recruits were looking to local heroes for inspiration and advice on equipment. Surfboard manufacturers began to see the merit of having good surfers endorsing their product. Surfing boomed and so did sales. Competition success began to equate to sales success, and the clever manufacturers hired the top surfers to work in their factories – Alan Byrne for Bob Davies Surfboards and Wayne Parkes for Atlas Woods, to name two. This had a minor effect at first as everyone was excited by any chance to make a living out of surfing – the perfect life!

The inherent problems of treating surfing as a competitive sport, and the encroachment of business interests on the competitions, led to gradual discontent with competitive surfing from about 1967 onwards. It is important to remember, however, that in 1967 the NZSRA had approximately 2000 members from an estimated surfing population of 15,000. There were a lot of people who were not interested in competitive surfing and who simply went to the beach for a few waves. Tony Reid: *'If we found out a competition was on at a beach, we would drive in the opposite direction knowing that there would be a few less surfers in the water.'*

The regional clubs did still serve a purpose. They were an excellent way of getting a ride to the surf as cars were still an expensive commodity and unavailable to many. Also, a lot of the new recruits to surfing were too young to drive – many a surfing memory revolves around a gremmy's first wild surf trips with the older surfers. The clubs began to get involved in zoning discussions at their local beaches, and in doing good works for the community in an effort to restore some of society's faith in surfers as human beings.

These administrative matters dragged surfers, rather unwillingly, back into the mainstream of sport. This was one reason that the clubs struggled to convince the bulk of surfers to join their ranks. Most still just wanted to go and ride the waves, and they had no need of belonging to a club for the sake of entering the nationals.

continued on page 84

Peter Way

John Paine described Peter as the Greg Noll of New Zealand surfing, referring to Greg Noll's notorious abilities in big Hawaiian surf and his embodiment of the surfing psyche when on land. Peter's input to New Zealand surfing covers the full spectrum of life saving, board riding, competition, board manufacture and administration. But it was his enjoyment and indulgence in surf lifestyle that is most remembered by his peers. He lived hard, partied hard and drove fast. I hope that some of the stories in this book will convey the skill and charm that was so obviously remembered by his peers.

Peter belonged to the North Piha Surf Life Saving Club and lived most of his early days at Piha. He attended every national surf life saving champs from 1954-76. Peter loved bodysurfing and riding surf skis with his cousin Barry Way, and friends Jim Palmer, Peter Byers, Butch Foubister and the rest of the young crew at North Piha. Peter remembers watching Rick Stoner and Bing Copeland paddling out from Camel Rock to the left-hander breaking on the bar. *'The clubbies wanted their blood for the impertinence of paddling out the back. The boys [Rick and Bing] took off and started to "broach" but then surfed along the face of the wave and kicked out. You could have heard a penny drop. Then the crowd went wild and we tried to order a board there and then.'* All of Peter's friends at the North Piha Surf Life Saving Club wanted to get boards – Mike Gardiner, Peter Russell-Green, Wayne Blundell, Ray Cates, Col Galligher, Ron Roman, Mel Sharples and Bob Ryan.

Peter's first board was a stringerless 9'6" shaped by Rick and Bing and finished by Peter Byers. They would take their new boards to surf carnivals at places such as Waipu, Muriwai, Karekare and Port Waikato. Peter Russell-Green was a tailor/cutter and he would turn large plastic bags into primitive wet suits for the North Piha surfers. They were adequate for keeping a football jersey dry underneath thus allowing a bit more surfing time.

PHOTO ALAN GODFERY

Peter's legendary confidence in the surf was built up by surf club mentors who took him out in big seas at Piha. He won a silver medal for bravery after he supported another man, for several hours, who had been swept out to sea by 10-15 foot surf at North Piha. No one had been able to swim out to the man but Peter managed it and supported the swimmer until another North Piha Surf Life Saving Club member arrived on a surf ski to take him in. They drifted a long way out to sea before any help could arrive and ended up nearly as far north as Bethells Beach. Peter had to swim back in on his own.

Together with Mike Gardiner and Phil 'Turkey' Delaney (and later Paul von Zalinski, Ron Roman and John Paine), Peter discovered most of the beaches around Pakiri and Mangawhai on the north-east coast of New Zealand, and was among the first to surf Whangamata and much of the Taranaki area. He began to go further afield for waves when John McDermott came over from Australia in 1962-63, and stayed with Peter. *'Easter 1963, we went to visit Mike Gardiner at Opunake in Mal Sharples' V8 Ford pickup. There was Turkey Delaney, John McDermott, Rex Banks and myself. Mick, Turk, Hermit and I started to paddle out at Sky Williams, in-coming tide, offshore howling, four foot and*

(above) Peter Way is New Zealand's leading surf legend. He is renowned for his surfing and surf life saving, his driving, his board building, and an ability to get up to mischief and excessive behaviour beyond the call of duty. He is shown mid-way through a cutback at a favourite break, Raglan, 1963.

(right) **Raglan again, well positioned on a good-sized day. Peter was very confident in big surf and excelled in these sorts of conditions.**

perfect. However, none of us got out — it just pumped, getting bigger with every wave. Sky Williams never closed out but it did that day at 20 foot plus! The next day I paddled out at Cemetery Point, just around from Opunake Beach, and it was 20 foot plus with the best conditions you could wish for.'

Peter surfed all the national surf champs up to 1968 and was first in the senior men's section of the inaugural nationals in 1963. He represented New Zealand at the world champs in Puerto Rico in 1968. *'The competitions were a good chance to surf some waves with only five or six others out. I remember getting excellent waves for the semis of the 68 champs at Kumara Patch and Stent Road.'*

When the new wave of young surfers came through in the mid-60s, Peter was there to act as a surfing mentor and, more importantly, a driver. Wayne Parkes, Peter Tremaine, Taff Kennings, Don Prince and Aussies Al Nichols and Mick Hopper were all regular recipients of Peter's surf hospitality, as were many others. It was this new surf crew who dubbed Peter 'Grandad'. He had a huge influence on these young surfers and inspired many to surf in conditions in which they might normally have hesitated.

Peter: *'We had a bit of rivalry going with Atlas Woods for board*

building. When we arrived at Piha one day, I saw Jacky Mitchell's Land Rover parked there. I went and got some fish off Peter Byers, who was on the beach, and stuffed it into the wheels, under the seats and in the air vent. Jacky told me it took weeks to find the one in the air vent and she had been driving with the windows down to get rid of the smell.'

Driving was another area in which Peter had a big reputation – the reputation depended on whether you were in the car with him or meeting him head-on while on the dirt roads. He drove a 38 Chevy and then an FJ Holden and did some stock car racing and hill climbs which honed his driving skills.

'I did 150,000 miles in 18 months in my FJ Holden, everywhere between Kaitaia and Bluff. I did lots of work on the engine and we could do 100mph down the motorway with eight boards up. It eventually had an old cane chair for the front seat and no back seat.'

Apart from being surfer, board builder, mentor and driver, Peter also made a mark in the administration of the sport. He was a founder member of North Reef Board Riders, then Windansea and was president of Windansea for a year. He was also involved for a short time with the New Zealand Surf Riders' Association.

Peter was a regular visitor to overseas shores and considers foreign influences to have been very important in the 60s. He spent time in Australia, California and Hawaii, and made good use of his Windansea contacts.

Peter moved to New Plymouth in the early 70s and stayed there until 1976 before leaving for Queensland where he lives today.

I'll leave the final words to Peter's contemporaries.

Wayne Parkes:

'There were two places that I felt really safe with Peter, in the water because he was such a good swimmer, and in a car because he was such a good driver. I would go out in surf that I might normally have hesitated over because Peter would inspire confidence. He was so strong in big surf. One time at Raglan, Peter was out on his own in huge surf, riding an 11' Scott Dillon gun, and I was standing on the rocks watching. His board washed up and I rescued it from getting battered on the rocks, then Peter swam in and shouted to me, "Just throw the f***ing thing back in. Throw it!" So I threw it as far as I could, it bounced off the rocks and into the water, Peter recovered it and off he paddled again into the distance.'

Bob Davie:

'He added so much to New Zealand surfing in his own way. There wouldn't be a surfer from that era in the Auckland area that didn't know Peter Way. He travelled the whole of New Zealand surfing and making surfboards. He was what you'd call today your bad grommet. We used to be scared to go to parties where he was going to be. You'd never know what was going to happen. Peter had this mate "Turkey" and they used to go to Raglan a lot. They had no money so on the way down they'd whip out the old piano wire with a lead weight on the end and knock a turkey off its roost at night, carry on down to The Point and cook it up.'

Dave Jackman:

'He was a great surfer and an excellent surf life saving competitor. He also loved to tell stories and hang out with the "boys". He spent plenty of time at the Takapuna pool hall, drinking and smoking. He was a bit caught up in the hype and popularity of surfing but he was a legend for the local surfers. He was always the one doing the extreme things and being reckless. He was the local hero. The younger surfers loved his image but people were also a bit nervous about him because he could be a bit too wild.'

Chas Lake:

'Peter and some friends trashed a room in the city where another surf associate was staying. During the mayhem, Peter came across a parrot-shaped bottle filled with a green liqueur. He smashed the top off the bottle on a table and proceeded to skull the bottle in one. Peter endlessly renewed himself by hanging out with the latest group of grommets. He truly kept in touch with the heart of the sport and was a role model whether he wished to be or not. He just continued to live the surfing life and was hard core before hard core was discovered.'

Don Prince:

'I always had a seat in the car, and Tram (Peter Tremaine) too. We were about 16 years old and Peter [Way] took us all over the North Island, exploring all sorts of new breaks. Peter had all the contacts. He took good care of all the young guys and nurtured their surfing. He would take us out in all conditions – it used to scare the pants off me sometimes but if worst came to worst, Peter was the sort of guy who could rescue you.

'These days you wouldn't get away with the sort of hooliganism we got up to. One night we towed the back seat of his FJ Holden from Kaitaia to Whangarei before cutting it loose on a one-way bridge – there were sparks all the way and the stuffing caught on fire. We used to take air rifles everywhere with us and shoot street lights, birds and the big inflatable Moggy men that they had outside gas stations.

'Piha Road was Peter's road. An A40 with fat tyres overtook him once and he just took off after it. Taff and I were in the back, with no seat, and we were getting tossed all over the place. Peter caught him up and started bumping him until he did a 180 degree spin off the road. Peter screeched to a halt, backed up and just snarled at the poor bewildered driver before driving off again at a nice gentle pace.'

Andy McAlpine:

'Peter jumped on the tractor attached to the pie cart in Hamilton and just drove off with it. We were left rolling with laughter while the owner shouted at him from inside the cart. He was lucky he wasn't arrested for that one. He did so many wild things.'

(above) Peter was able to support his surfing lifestyle by building boards and selling them from his Takapuna factory, and through a string of agents around the country. This stylish ad is from 1968.

PHOTO BEV BREWARD COLLECTION

PHOTO NEVILLE MASTERS

(top left) **Bev Breward during a trip to California in 1964.** *'I was surfing Malibu and I think Leroy Grannis, the famous surf photographer, took this picture.'*

(above) **Joan Atherton at Taipa, Northland, 1965.** *'I couldn't really swim so I never went out above chest-high in the water. I was usually on small waves but I loved to ride the nose.'*

PHOTO TRISH DWYER COLLECTION

PHOTO TRISH DWYER COLLECTION

(above, l to r) **Raewyn St George, Joan Paton, Trish Dwyer, New Plymouth, 1966.**

(right, l to r) **Trish Dwyer, Robyn Gothard and Doria Gothard, Foxton picnic, 1966.** Trish: *'I started surfing on an Atlas Woods bought from Dave Littlejohn. Then I ordered a Del. I had heard a bit about the Australians in town and when Nigel [Dwyer] delivered my new board, I thought he was pretty cool.'*

Girls can do anything ...

Not all the women stayed on the beach watching the men surf. Around 1959, Peter Miller's sister Marilyn was riding a longboard that Peter had built. She surfed it around Napier and Wellington and was a true novelty in the late 1950s. By 1961 Joan Atherton was riding a home-made Malibu board at Ninety Mile Beach, Bev Breward was riding an Australian-made Malibu in Christchurch and Cindy Webb was getting her first waves at Whangamata on an Australian-made Malibu. There were few others, that I have been able to discover, that surfed in the early 1960s and none that I know of who built boards.

Women have always been a minority in surfing and I believe one of the reasons is the sheer physical strength required for learning to surf. This was particularly true when trying to negotiate the surf on the big Malibu boards of the early 60s. On the other hand, the boards were very stable and could be ridden in small, manageable surf, so anyone who persevered would be rewarded with waves. In direct contradiction to this are the observations of Lyn Humphreys who took up surfing around 1962 in Taranaki: *'I started surfing at Opunake Beach when I was 13 years old. Someone arrived with a surfboard that summer and it was all go from there. We scoured the countryside looking for old boards. There were just about as many girls as guys surfing then – I surfed with Kerry Lines, Carolyn Robinson, Yvonne McCall, Marg Harvey and Sandra Caverhill. We'd go surfing with Stew Newport and Tommy Waite, and go anywhere around the Taranaki coast that was going off.*

'The guys and gals got on like one big family. We loved each other's company. I remember one time when we travelled to Wellington, the locals at The Corner (Lyall Bay) were surprised to see women, Kerry Lines and me, out surfing let alone getting some good waves.'

Lyn was an Opunake Surf Life Saving Club member before she took up surfing and she maintained both pursuits. *'My first surfboard was a dunger from hell but then I bought a 9'4" Quane double stringer from Dave Littlejohn who was one of the real mentors of surfing in New Plymouth.'*

New Plymouth appears to have been unique in terms of the number of women who were surfing. Aside from those mentioned by Lyn Humphreys, Trish Dwyer (who began surfing in 1963 on a board made by local surfer Gig Bailey) was surfing with fellow converts Diane Saywell, Cheryl Whicombe, Tiddy Walker and Suzie Curzons.

At the 1963 nationals there was no women's event because of the lack of women surfers. By 1964, however, sufficient women had taken up the sport to run an event and Cindy Webb showed what three years' experience could do for a surfer. *'In 1963, I left school and got a job, and was able to buy my first surfboard, a Roger Land 9'3". I had been borrowing a board for a year and a half so the thrill of finally owning my own board was enormous.*

'There was only a handful of women surfers ("femlins", as some called us) in 1963-64. Not all the young women were interested in getting up at dawn to go surfing, and getting sunburnt and developing bumpy knees from paddling. We also surfed right through winter with no wetsuits so it took a very hardy soul to be a surfer but I was totally committed. It was a pioneering time and I experienced some resentment from the carefully groomed women who stayed on the beach, because I was out surfing with their boyfriends, but I was too interested in surfing and spent all my time in the water anyway. I got pretty weather beaten.

'I won the women's section of the nationals in 1964 and 65. The contests were relaxed and friendly – a good chance to meet the few other women who were surfing. Back in the city, they asked me if I had had a nice weekend waterskiing!'

Around 1963, Jonette Mead took up surfing after watching some visiting American surfers getting tubed on the bar at Whangamata. *'I was 13 years old and felt an overwhelming urge to surf like that. I borrowed a red "Gidget" surfboard from the Whangamata Surf Life Saving Club and set about learning to surf. I found out I was a goofy footer so the Whanga Bar suited me perfectly.'*

Jonette's first board was a second-hand 9'9" Atlas Woods

(above) The finalists of the women's section of the 1964 nationals, Mount Maunganui. **(l to r)** Cindy Webb, Unknown, Unknown, Jacky Mitchell, Pauline Thomson, Gail Patty.

(left) Dave Walpole presents Cindy Webb with the prize for the first woman in the 1964 nationals – an Atlas Woods surfboard. Cindy: *'The contests were relaxed and friendly – a good chance to meet the few other women who were surfing. Back in the city, they asked me if I had had a nice weekend waterskiing!'*

(below) Cindy Webb cruising her way to victory in the 1965 nationals at Fitzroy Beach, New Plymouth.

(right, I to r) **Christina Meister, Jonette Mead, Cindy Webb.** Posing for a 'girls can do it too' article following the 1964 nationals.

PHOTO CINDY WEBB COLLECTION

(right) **Jonette Mead at Whangamata, 1964.**
'Manu Bay was one of my favourite surf spots – sharing waves with friends and mentors Cindy Webb, Peter McAllum, Bob Comer, Roger Land, Peter Miller and Lauri "Curly" Pinniger. As the 60s progressed, we were joined in the surf by Jill McGregor, Leslie Parkinson, Jill McNaughton, Karen Kneebone and Sue Hodkinson.'

PHOTO JONETTE MEAD COLLECTION

which she shared with her brother. It was very heavy and had a little red devil which her brother had painted on it. Jonette became a member of Raglan's Point Board Riders' Club where she surfed with Cindy Webb. Jonette quickly became a skilled surfer as demonstrated by her second placing in the 1965 nationals at New Plymouth.

Jonette surfed mainly at Raglan and Whangamata and she was one of the first surfers to visit Onemana Beach, north of Whangamata, when it was still farmland and they had to ask permission to go through to the beach.

'Being a woman surfer in those early days was great. I suddenly had a whole lot of new surfing brothers and got to surf with my father [Ray Mead] *and my brother* [Peter Mead]. *Everyone was great, shared waves and didn't give me a hard time.'*

Gail Patty and her sister Joan lead the charge for women's surfing in Gisborne. Gail started surfing in 1963 when she was on surf life saving patrol. *'I pinched a guy's board when he fell off and had a go while he swam in.'* She converted to surfing and gave away the surf life saving: *'I rescued more people on a board than as a surf life saver.'* Gail surfed with all the Gisborne locals, including sister Joan, Marice Richardson and Marcia Rowles. *'I got good respect from the Gissy boys but I had to be assertive. Generally the girls got a hard time. I remember swinging my board into one guy who had received three warnings about dropping in.'*

Gail was a formidable competitor, winning all the local and regional contests (with Joan usually second), and winning the nationals in 1967. *'It was a highlight winning the nationals fair and square despite one competitor attempting to influence the judges. I also thought it was great that my sister Joan made the semi-finals of the 1967 nationals when she was four-and-a-half months pregnant.*

'Roberts Road was a favourite spot for its quality and proximity to home and work. I didn't travel far outside Gisborne, except for contests at Mount Maunganui, Whangamata, New Plymouth and Christchurch, until I went overseas in the late 60s – there was no need. One of my best memories still is perfect right-handers at

Makarori centre – locked in, covered up and hand trails.'

Lois Clark, wife of Ken Clark who worked for Atlas Woods, was another woman who got off to an early start as a surfer in New Zealand – around 1963. She had Ken make her a board into which he glassed black lace. It was her pride and joy even if the board was a bit heavy. *'I always got looks of admiration for the board and had no trouble selling it – at a profit! Family commitments eventually prevented me from going surfing and I suspect this happened to a number of surfers who became mothers.'*

In the early to mid-60s, the men were very accepting of women surfers and treated them as equals in the surf. However, as the surf became more crowded and competition for waves increased, women started to feel the pressure.

Jonette Mead: *'The first time I ever surfed to my right, which I found very difficult, I was about to go left on a right-hander. On each side of me was a male surfer from hell – big, tough Graham Dunne from Australia, who glared at me, and on the other side was Peter Way, board builder and surf nazi, who also glared at me. I went right, no sweat, under such a threat. Lots of stuff happened in national contests, like the women's heats were put out at the end of the day in low-tide, on-shore mush, while the best surf was reserved for the men's divisions. I created the women-only Sunsmart Women's Open Surfing Champs as a result of that.'*

Cindy Webb: *'When I started surfing, the men generally respected my dedication to the surf and I was rarely hassled or dropped in on. However, when I was New Zealand Champion in 1965, I was contacted by the NZSRA to say they had three return trips to the world titles in San Diego and that I should get ready to go along to represent New Zealand. I went out and acquired a passport and had my smallpox vaccination, and then I heard from the NZSRA that one airfare was no longer available, so I would not be going! Only the Senior Men's and Junior Men's Champions would go.'*

Jacky Mitchell: *'Being a woman surfer was not an issue when I first started around 1963-64. Surfers were an oddity and a woman surfer was odder still. I did feel a bit looked down on for my strong*

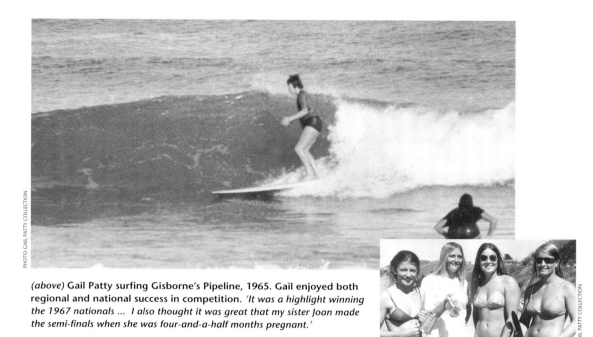

(*above*) **Gail Patty surfing Gisborne's Pipeline, 1965. Gail enjoyed both regional and national success in competition. 'It was a highlight winning the 1967 nationals ... I also thought it was great that my sister Joan made the semi-finals when she was four-and-a-half months pregnant.'**

(*right, l to r*) **Unknown, unknown, Gail Patty, Cindy Webb. Winners of a 1966 Gisborne Board Riders open contest.**

(*left*) **Women finalists for the 1966 nationals at Gisborne (l to r) Jonette Mead, Cindy Webb, Pauline Thomson, Gail Patty, Janette Murdoch (winner), Joan Patty.**

PHOTO TIM MURDOCH

PHOTO TIM MURDOCH

(above and left) **The face of the future – Val Tredrea was a strong surfer on the short boards of the late 60s, and went on to win the women's division of the 1969 and 1971 nationals.**

involvement in a male-dominated sport. Gender only became a problem when the surf became more crowded and strength and aggression started to dictate the number of waves you could get. Physically it is harder for women to surf as the upper body strength is not as great so they sit out there a lot longer and end up dropping in because they get sick and tired of waiting. We would either make it and look great or totally blow it and take someone's head off in the process.'

Jacky started surfing at the age of 14 at Ninety Mile Beach. *'Dad* [Atlas Woods owner Alan Mitchell] *handed me a large ironing board, so I thought, and said, "You stand up on it when the waves push you in." He was right.'*

The Mitchell family lived on Takapuna Beach where Jacky surfed with the likes of Wayne Parkes, Steve King and Taff Kennings. *'There were mutterings about me hanging out with the surf boys just to jump in the bushes with them but that was not true. My big aim was to get to the world titles. I entered the 1968 nationals to test myself against the other surfers and to get to the*

PHOTO TIM MURDOCH

(above) **Jacky Mitchell at North Piha, 1968. Jacky went on to victory at the 1968 nationals held at Christchurch.**

world titles. I didn't really know the other women surfers that well but I enjoyed the competition for what it was and I won.'

Jacky travelled to Puerto Rico for the 1968 world titles and she was joined there by Penny Whiting (now famous for her sailing exploits). Penny was a keen surfer and member of the infamous Surf Syndicate. She was determined to make it to Puerto Rico to represent New Zealand at the world champs so she saved enough money to get to Hawaii and got a job as a caretaker at Makaha. Penny practised surfing every day while earning her fare to Puerto Rico. She didn't place at the world champs but she made some good contacts and spent two years as a professional judge at surf competitions in California.

Exploration seems to be in the blood of all surfers and the women were no exception. Joan Atherton, and husband Bob, opened up most of the surf breaks in the Far North; Lyn Humphreys explored most of the Taranaki coastline and travelled the length of the North Island to surf and compete; Bev Breward travelled to Hawaii on her own in 1964 for a four month working/surfing holiday; Gail Patty travelled to Australia and California in the late-60s and early 70s; and Cindy Webb travelled all over New Zealand, often with Jonette Mead and Christina Meister, surfing and competing.

With the rapid rise in popularity of surfing in the mid-60s, a lot more women got involved in the sport but, in the words of Cindy Webb, *'Unfortunately, the increase in women surfing did not keep pace with the increase in males surfing and more than ever it became a male-dominated sport.'*

Val Tredrea stepped into the competitive arena in the late 60s and seemed to be the standard bearer for women surfers and the new shortboards. Other strong contenders were the cranch sisters from Piha. However, as the quote from Cindy Webb indicates, more men than women were entering the sport and the strong presence that women had in surfing in the early 60s, particularly in places such as Taranaki, slowly diminished. The ratio of male to female surfers has probably still not improved to this day.

continued on page 91

Roger Land

Roger was working for Fisher and Paykel in 1961 when a workmate showed him a sketch he had picked up in Australia of how to build a surfboard. This sparked an interest in surfing for Roger and seemed to offer a way out of the office job he had held for three years. He started building surfboards in his parents' backyard in Auckland under the 'Roland' (ROgerLAND) name.

Roger spent as much time as possible in the surf and gathered as much information as he could on board building. He surfed Piha, Raglan, Mount Maunganui, Whangamata and all the main breaks of the early 60s, and he surfed with the same few surfers who were around in those early years, such as Peter Way, Peter Byers, Tim Murdoch and John Paine. *'There were only three to four guys at any beach in those days.'*

A passion for deer hunting took Roger to the South Island in 1963 but on his return to Auckland, he continued to make surfboards for which he gained a good reputation. His boards were well shaped and finished, and looked good.

In 1963-64, in order to be closer to Raglan, Roger moved to Hamilton and set up a board factory. He joined the Point Board Riders Club straight away and settled into surfing Raglan on a regular basis. *'Alan Godfery and I had been frequent visitors to Hamilton anyway, making the most of the surf at Raglan and the notorious parties the Hamilton gang organised.'*

Roger stayed on in Hamilton for 18 months, then he moved his business to Gisborne in 1964-65. He moved back to Hamilton and a new factory in 1965. However, the business took off too quickly and ran into cash flow problems. Roger sold the business at the end of 1965 and moved to Rotorua to work on fibreglass boats.

Soon after, Bob Davie asked him to come over to Mount Maunganui and shape for him so Roger found himself working the week in Rotorua then driving to the Mount to shape

PHOTO BOB COMER

(above) Roger Land in 'Quasimodo' pose on the balcony of the old Whangamata Surf Life Saving Club, 1964.

PHOTO ALAN GODFERY

(above) Roger waving to photographer Alan Godfery, Piha, 1963.

PHOTO ROGER LAND

(left) Nigel Dwyer holding a balsa board built for Steve King, outside Roger Land's base of operations in Gisborne, 1965. Nigel was a glasser for Roger while in Gisborne. *'When business was slow, Roger and I went scrub cutting. We worked solidly for a couple of weeks but then we heard that Makarori Point was breaking, and I looked at Roger and said, "What are we doing here?". We just bailed out and went to the beach.'*

CUSTOM SURFBOARDS

LAND

ALEXANDRA ST.   HAMILTON PH 83-297

(above and left) A brochure for Land Surfboards showing prices and specifications.

PRICE LIST

Up to 9'3" £36 0 0
9'4" to 9'8" £38 0 0
9'9" to 10'0" £42 0 0
Guns, Bellyboards, Paddleboards etc.
on quote.

TRADE-IN'S ACCEPTED

CONSTRUCTION

The above prices include the following features:

* High Density CO₂ blown polyurethane foam.
* Double layer 10 ounce glass cloth with FOUR layers on rails.
* Extra glass around nose.
* New formula polyester Resins.
* Single hardwood stringer.
* 3 colour 15 layer all fibreglass skeg.
* Custom shaped to your specifications using latest techniques.
* Hand polished rails.
* Clear finish with small design.

EXTRAS

Additional stringers, Balsa or Redwood .... 20/- ea.
Extra cuts in foam .... 10/- per cut
Laminated tailblocks 15/-
T-Band stringers 40/-
Full design 20/-
Extra knee patch 10/-

REPAIRS

Supply and replace skeg £2 10 0
Reglass .... on quotation
Re Resin (depnding on condition £5 0 0
Nose blocks £2 0 0
Other repairs .... on quotation

* We specialise in high quality custom boards for both beginners and experienced riders.

surfboards in the weekend. *'When people wanted the latest fashion in surfboards, whatever it was, I was good at interpreting that and shaping what they wanted.'* He got sick of living inland and after getting married in 1967, he moved to Mount Maunganui to work fulltime for Bob Davie.

Roger and his wife moved back to Auckland in 1968, to save money to travel overseas. They departed for Hawaii at the end of 1968, and during the years 1969-71 Roger worked as a shaper for Sunset Surfboards in Hawaii, G&S in California (where he got a good reputation and started getting his own clientele) and SurfJet in New York, a rich-kid operation that covered 20,000 square feet and supplied the East Coast surfers. Roger also visited and surfed Mexico, Canada, England, Scotland and France.

Roger was one of the most dedicated and proficient shapers of the 60s, and his skills were well appreciated when he travelled the world. After his return to New Zealand in 1971, he shaped for Bob Davie, Nev Hines, Custom Design and Brian Weaver, not to mention producing his own backyard boards from Mairangi Bay. He still surfs occasionally and has recently made a return to the shaping bay to produce some boards for Surfline in Ruakaka.

(right) Roger Land surfing towards 'The Blowhole' at Mount Maunganui, 1963. This is another example of a very early water shot.

PHOTO DAVE WALPOLE

The paraphernalia

As surfing became more popular, the associated goods and services increased in number and quality. Surfing became big business and there were more ways to make money out of it than merely building surfboards.

Lights, camera, action!

The first 'add-on' to surfing to arrive in New Zealand was probably the surf movie. By 1957 Bud Browne had brought the first true surf movies to New Zealand (*Surfing in Hawaii* and *Riding the Big Surf*). Tim Murdoch ensured a steady supply of surf movies after that, the most popular being Bruce Brown's *The Endless Summer* which toured the country in 1965-66. It was the success of *The Endless Summer*, and the appearance of local surf breaks in the movie, that helped surfing take off as a sport.

Larry Keating was a young surfer from Titahi Bay in 1966: '*Tim Murdoch toured* The Endless Summer *and gave me a job on the road with it. I idolised Robert August and Mike Hynson, the two stars of the film. It gave me a chance to get around the country and surf breaks I had heard about. I saw the film hundreds of times and never got sick of it. It was because of that tour that I became involved in film and television, as I am now. Tim really inspired me in that direction.*'

In 1966-67, Tim Murdoch also produced his own feature film entitled *Out of the Blue* which was shot in New Zealand and Hawaii and starred Wayne Parkes. He followed this with *Seven Sundays* which was released in 1970. The only other full length movie produced locally during the 60s was Andy McAlpine's *Children of the Sun*, also shot around 1966-67. It features a great array of local breaks and surfers, and culminates in some impressive footage from Queensland's points with Wayne Parkes and George Greenough.

Andy McAlpine: '*I started surfing at Piha around the mid-60s, when I was about 17. Tim McLean and I hired boards from Peter Byers, the last of which I finally returned about 1998.*

'*I got inspired to make* Children of the Sun *after seeing a surf movie at Milford. I was working as a factory apprentice and thought a surfing career was much more attractive. I also wanted to show everyone how great surfing was. I made* Children of the Sun *first, then* Beautiful Day *with John Cassidy in the early 70s.*

'*Whangamata was one of my favourite breaks and I particularly liked Russell Hughes' surfing. He was one of the first to "climb and drop" on waves – a preview of short board moves.*'

Movies from overseas were the first source of offshore influence for many surfers. The movies predated the arrival of surf magazines in New Zealand and, in the absence of other information, showed our fledgling surfers what could be done on the waves. John Logan: '*The Aussies and the movies arrived in Gisborne at about the same time and we suddenly realised what could be done on a wave.* Surfing Hollow Days *showed at the local intermediate school hall and afterwards we were all just raving about what we had seen. It also woke us up to surfing reefs and*

(above) **Tim Murdoch and Andy McAlpine were the two locals who attempted to make commercially successful surf movies. Many amateur 8mm movies were shot but few had the inclination to attempt 16mm movies due to the cost and expertise required.**

(below) **Tim Murdoch armed with his movie camera.**

points, not just the beach breaks.' Even the notorious Gidget movies helped recruit new surfers, and give surfing a sense of being a legitimate sport.

The movies also gave local surfers a sense of being part of a worldwide 'brotherhood' in spite of New Zealand's isolation. They confirmed that surfers were 'cool' and unintentionally offered style advice for both in and out of the water.

Making the scene with a magazine ...

Overseas surf magazines began to arrive in the country in the baggage of foreign surfers who visited our shores from 1960 onwards. These treasures would be pounced upon by the local surfers and devoured from cover to cover. Board builders frequently used foreign surf magazines as inspiration for new designs. Photos were studied for ideas on how to surf and surf fashion was quickly replicated to the best possible degree.

It was not long before photos of New Zealand began to appear in the magazines courtesy of local surf photographers such as Alan Godfery and Tim Murdoch, and visiting photographers such as John Severson.

The first local magazine was published by Kevin Brightwell in April 1965. It was called *New Zealand Surfer* but changed to *New Zealand Surf Magazine* after one issue. The publication survived for six issues (just over one year) and covered a wide array of local surf events and locations, for example, the discovery of Goat Island Bay and Great Barrier Island. The next attempt at a magazine was not made until December 1968 with the publication of *Surfing New Zealand*. The small size of New Zealand's surfing population meant that the local surf magazines would always struggle.

A highlight of local surf publishing in the 60s was Wayne Warwick's *A Guide to Surfriding in New Zealand*, first published in 1965. Wayne grew up in Titahi Bay, near Wellington, where he was involved with the surf life saving club. He began surfing in his early teens around 1962-3. He was an avid traveller and explorer, and would disappear for weekends, returning with stories of newly discovered breaks. He got a job as a sales rep for Viking/Seven Seas Publishing and while travelling the country on their behalf, took the opportunity to check plenty of surf spots and meet the locals. *A Guide to Surfriding in New Zealand* was a result of all those travels. The book was originally compiled at a time when everyone was quite willing to offer information about their surf spots. (Information was not so forthcoming for the second edition in the 1970s.) I have a particular admiration for Wayne Warwick, having been a regular user of the second edition of his guide, and for his efforts to capture some of New Zealand's surfing history within the guide.

(below right) The first issue of *New Zealand Surfer* from April 1965. Kevin Brightwell was the publisher, and the cover and centre spread photos were taken by Bob Comer who was staff photographer for the magazine.

(below) *Surfing New Zealand* was first published in December 1968 but it only lasted a few issues.

Surf music

With many of our first visitors coming from California, the surf music of The Beach Boys, Dick Dale and the like soon infiltrated the country, probably before the radio stations began to play it. As the 60s progressed and the hippy lifestyle blossomed, surfers were in the forefront of importing the new music to New Zealand, particularly the English vanguard such as The Beatles and The Rolling Stones. Being avid travellers, and given the alternative nature of the surfing lifestyle, it was no surprise that surfers were quick to 'tune in, turn on and drop out'. Travellers returning to New Zealand came armed with the music of Jimi Hendrix, The Doors, Jefferson Airplane and all the other icons of the late 60s, and they introduced them to the surf community of New Zealand. Once again, they were probably ahead of radio or TV in introducing hippy lifestyle and music to the country.

Graham Gantley: *'The drug thing really kicked in during the late 60s and then into the 70s. That was largely due to travelling surfers returning with new music and ideas. We were listening to Hendrix and The Doors and all those people long before they were released in New Zealand.'*

One radio station was strongly associated with the surf community. Radio Hauraki began its days as a pirate station broadcasting from a ship in the Hauraki Gulf so it had a style that fitted well with surfing. DJ Ian Magan hosted a new show for the summer of 1967-68 called 'Surf Scene 67' and the station was involved in sponsoring surf events.

The surf clubs were also well known for their raucous parties or 'rages'. Gisborne Board Riders was particularly well known for its rages after competitions held there. One party required 2000 milkshake cartons for drinks, a beer tanker with 16 taps (which were kept busy all night), and a band from Auckland by the name of Killing Floor who played in Chicago brass style. (The aftermath of this party featured in a famous photograph in the *Truth* newspaper which confirmed all the long-held prejudices that surfers were hooligans.) A local Gisborne band called Crazy Urge played at several Gisborne Board Riders rages and had a

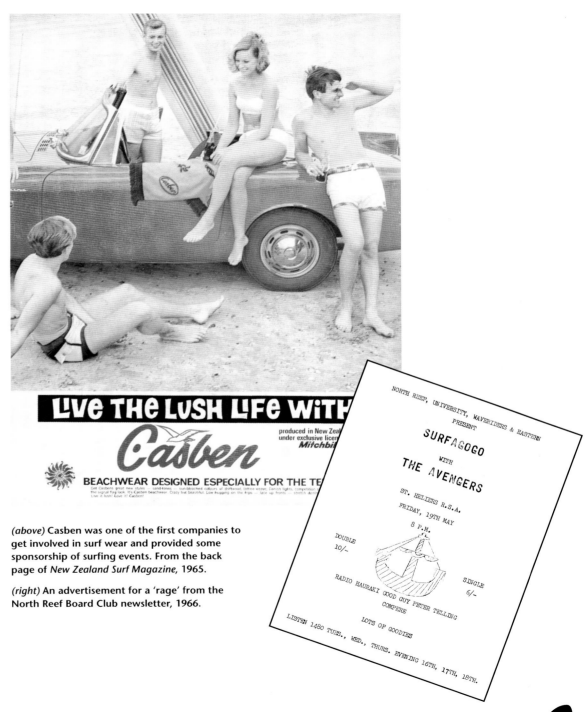

(above) Casben was one of the first companies to get involved in surf wear and provided some sponsorship of surfing events. From the back page of *New Zealand Surf Magazine*, 1965.

(right) An advertisement for a 'rage' from the North Reef Board Club newsletter, 1966.

MADE IN N.Z. BY HOLEPROOF

(right) Shot at that curious hotbed of surfing, Takapuna Beach, Aywon show the style that they thought surfers might go for in 1970.

(below) The Sundowners in action at 'Le Mount Cabaret', Mount Maunganui, as part of the celebrations surrounding the selection of Miss Surf Queen 1963. (l to r) Ted Toi, Dave Abrahams, Max Purdie, Sonny Day (obscured), Lloyd Te Ngaio, Bob Wynard, Dave Henry.

repertoire that included Cream and Jimi Hendrix. The Sundowners was another local band that played covers of surf music, the current pop music, and a couple of originals, at such venues as 'Le Mount Cabaret', Mount Maunganui.

The closest thing to indigenous surf music probably came when the band, Music Convention, composed the sound track for *Children of the Sun*. It was still heavily influenced by the music from *The Endless Summer* but it was original.

Surf clothing

It is ironic that clothing sales are the fuel of the modern surf industry yet surf clothing was unknown in New Zealand in the early 60s. Some surf fashion had arrived in the country with visiting foreign surfers but it was promptly acquired, by fair means or foul, by local surfers. Visiting surfers were surprised to see the locals still surfing in the the 60s equivalent of Speedos. The foreign magazines showed some surf fashions (which were copied by locals, for example, Bob Comer's mother running up board shorts for Bob and his friends) but none of the overseas

products were available in New Zealand and no one was interested in, or able, to import them.

Bob Davie was one of the first to introduce locally made surf clothing to his shop. In the summer of 1966-67, he began selling T-shirts on which was printed the logo for Bob Davies Surfboards. *'Getting clothing that was a little different from the run-of-the-mill was the hardest part. There was no realisation amongst the clothing manufacturers of the potential of surf clothing. Things changed quickly, however, as Hang Ten and other surf labels became available. Anything that the average person in the street was not wearing was OK with the surfers.'*

Denis Quane introduced a range of clothing at pretty much the same time as Bob. Quane Surfboards sold T-shirts, hooded sweatshirts and board shorts out of the showrooms in front of the factory at Redcliffs, Christchurch. Denis also had a Quane-brand wetsuit made from a laminated foam. Around 1967-68, Denis also employed Bob Tulloch to travel New Zealand in a van supplied by Quane Surfboards, setting up agents to sell boards, clothing, wax and ding kits (a dedicated surf rep, maybe the first!). Denis opened his first Quane surf shop in the city in 1968-69. Bob Tulloch ran this shop, and split-knee cords and leather sandals were added to the range, followed by Wrangler jeans.

However, the surfboard manufacturers were not the only ones cashing in on surf clothing. 'Live the Lush Life ...' read the *New Zealand Surf Magazine* back cover ad for Casben swimwear in 1966. They were producing swimwear especially for the surf market and marketing specifically to young males. Polaroid got in on the act too, advertising their glasses with surf themes on the 'Surfing with the Star' page of the *Auckland Star*. The Wellington branch of clothing store Vance Vivian also ran a promotion for the summer of 1966-67 that included a fashion parade of Catalina surf wear and a 'colour movie of the Catalina-sponsored Long Beach Surf Club at the World Championships in Peru'.

As the 60s came to a close, the overseas clothing labels (such as Hang Ten) began to take over the local market and little has changed to this day.

PHOTO MIKE McGLYNN

(previous page) see caption on page 112.

PHOTO GAIL PATTY COLLECTION

(above) Gail Patty surfing at Noosa Heads, Australia 1968. The short board revolution was born out of these perfect Queensland points and took the surfing world by storm over the next decade.

PHOTO GEORGE GREENOUGH

(above) Wayne Parkes surfing Point Cartwright, Queensland, Australia 1966. The photo was taken by George Greenough who was a major protagonist in the radical redesign of boards dubbed the 'shortboard revolution'.

(right) These two McTavish-inspired, V-bottom boards from 1968, shaped by Roger Land, clearly show the direction in which board design was going at the end of the 60s – shorter.

PHOTO ROGER LAND

By the summer of 1967-68, a certain maturity had established itself in the surf industry. A number of board manufacturers, such as Atlas Woods, Bob Davie and Quane, were working to full capacity to service the seemingly insatiable demand for boards. A strong administration for surfing was in place, as evidenced by the number of local competitions and the strength of the national championship. There were also plenty of 'add-ons' becoming available in the form of clothing, magazines, movies and music. Surfing was becoming more accepted in mainstream society as a legitimate sport and not just a haven for anti-establishment louts. Surfing even made it onto the television and radio.

Although filmed about six years before its debut on New Zealand TV in 1968, the screening of *Surf's Up* was a real coup for surfers and probably the first time many had seen surfing on TV. Ian Magan of Radio Hauraki was also up with the times when he hosted a new show for the summer of 1967-68 called 'Surf Scene 67'.

The hippy revolution of the late 60s was poised to hit the country and travelling surfers were at the forefront of importing the associated music, behaviour and 'look'. However, the biggest shake up of all was to occur inside the sport of surfing itself.

Talkin' 'bout a revolution ...

In 1967, on the Queensland coast, Bob McTavish, George Greenough and Nat Young began experimenting with shorter surfboards. They began by cutting down from 9'3" boards to around 8'6", then quickly chopped down again to around 7'6" and less. They were also experimenting with new shapes and fins, and within a year virtually every board manufacturer was producing shortboards – the Malibu had become dormant (not extinct as we are now discovering).

Wayne Parkes was travelling to Australia most winters in the late 1960s and, as a shaper in Bob McTavish's Sydney factory, he was right in amongst the shortboard revolution. *'In 1966, I travelled to Hawaii and California, then on to Sydney where I met Bob McTavish at his board factory. McTavish was a leading shaper in Australia at that time and I was really lucky because he let me work with him. I was able to learn so much from McTavish because he didn't see me as competition for the Australian surfing market. He knew I would be going back to New Zealand and he was happy for me to take his design ideas home. The following year [1967], I went to Sydney again and had another huge learning experience with McTavish. There was enormous experimentation going on with the shape and length of boards and I remember regular visits to the factory by Nat Young and Peter Drouyn. I was also working alongside legends like George Greenough, Russell Hughes, Kevin Platt and Algie Grudd. McTavish would leave me to finish off shaping his boards while he went surfing.'*

Thus, New Zealand was introduced to the shortboard faster than most countries and it was adopted as the new direction in shaping very quickly. Steve King: *'What transpired back in New Zealand was that all the boards we'd built through the winter for the summer selling season were obsolete overnight.'*

This radical new direction in board design inspired a new wave of board builders to start up, for example, Hannah Surfboards (Hastings), Brian Weaver (Auckland) and Jackman Way (Auckland). Surfboards Gisborne was started in 1968-69 by Gary Lidgard (shaper), Benny Hutchings (glasser) and Bill Carson (glasser), the first board manufacturer in Gisborne since the departure of Bob Davie in 1966-67. Blanks were supplied by Peter Byers and templates came from Bob McTavish.

The shortboard revolution also meant a revolution in riding style – nose riding was dead and 'vertical performance' became the way to surf. Wayne Parkes: *'They started doing re-entries up in Queensland in 66. Guys like Peter Drouyn knew how to do them while the rest were still straightening out and going round sections. You really had to have those shorter boards to be able to try the new moves. Watching Nat [Young] surf on McTavish's boards was a huge influence.'*

The new boards were designed to be ridden much closer to the

(above) Advertisements for three of the smaller, local board shops that became the trend in the 70s. Surfers chose to have custom boards made by a local craftsman who knew the conditions and often knew the surfer's abilities.

PHOTO TIM MURDOCH

PHOTO TAFF KENNINGS COLLECTION

(above and right) Taff Kennings was one of the top contest surfers during the 60s. He represented New Zealand in the Tasman Bucket contest in Australia, and was a founder member of the North Reef and Windansea surf clubs. He also wrote the 'Surfing with the Star' column for the *Auckland Star* newspaper. As the surf in New Zealand became more crowded, towards the end of the 60s, the lure of exotic locations led Taff to Australia, Mexico and Hawaii where he lived and surfed.

critical breaking section of the wave and there was a lot more cutting back to the power generated there. With more activity occurring on the wave, it was also important to have the wave to yourself. The sharing of waves, common with Malibu riding, faded away and 'dropping in' became increasingly frowned upon.

Young riders who changed to shortboards early, or who started out on shortboards, started to shine in the competitions leading to a revolution in the competitive ranks (although no one could knock Wayne Parkes off his perch until he retired from competition after the 1970 nationals). Surfers such as Graham Gantley, Benny Hutchings and Kevin Jarrett began to appear amongst the leaders, and Alan Byrne was a successful convert to shortboards.

Although the transition to shortboards was quite rapid, it didn't all happen at once. Surf articles in late 1967 were still referring to shorter boards of 9' to 9'4". However, by 1968 Peter Way was riding two boards at 7'10" and 8'3", respectively, and by 1969, 6'6" to 6'10" was the norm with square tails, thick rails and weighing around 5-7 pounds. 'S' decks were in and pin tails were on the way.

With boards getting smaller from 1967 onwards, younger surfers were better able to manage the equipment and get into surfing. The number of surfers rose quickly in the late 1960s to a point where Tim Murdoch estimated that there were 22,000 surfers in 1969.

Disillusionment with competition

Despite the surge in the number of new surfers, relatively few could be attracted into the surf clubs. Most were happy not to compete or realised that they were not capable of competing. The other benefits of club life from the early to mid-60s – as a source of transport to the waves and moral support in a rather outcast sport – were negated by a greater pool of surfers to scrounge rides from, greater access to vehicles and a degree of mainstreaming in the sport. Interest in the clubs, therefore, tended to be confined to those who wished to be in the nationals or who wanted to hang out with the top competitors.

The surf clubs began in 1962 with the establishment first of North Reef Board Club (Takapuna) then Point Board Riders (Raglan), followed by Mount Maunganui Board Riders and Surf City Board Riders (New Plymouth) in 1963. Thereafter, there was a surge in clubs being established to a peak of 28 clubs represented at the 1967 nationals.

Surfers such as John Paine, Taff Kennings, Tim Murdoch and Peter Fitzsimmons, who all wrote for the newspapers, frequently scolded the readers for their lack of commitment to the clubs. However, most surfers knew they could go surfing whether they belonged to a club or not and if they had no desire to compete then they saw no incentive to join.

Who was the winner on the day?

The staunchest supporters of the clubs were those who competed in the nationals and other regional competitions around the country. The competitions were attractive, not only for the glory but for economic reasons as well. Board manufacturers supported good surfers in the hope that their victories would result in more sales.

By 1967, there were already complaints that the competitions were not necessarily a fair reflection of the best surfing talent, and that some surfers consistently won in order to keep

continued on page 101

Wayne Parkes

Wayne is one of New Zealand's most influential surfers. He was virtually unbeatable during a competitive career spanning 1965-1970, and his shaping career spans 1965 to the present day. He epitomised the young surfer of the 60s with skills and attitude to match.

Wayne started surfing at Takapuna Beach, in 1962, when he was 12 years old. With friends Steve King and Roddy Allison, he would surf on anything he could get hold of including Lilos and pieces of wood. *'The first real surfboard I saw was when some woman, who I didn't know, brought one down to Takapuna Beach. I managed to get a go on the board and I was amazed at what it could do.'*

Wayne's first board, a Wilson & Edwards, cost £26. *'I ran pamphlets, and sold old bottles and scrap metal to pay for it. It seemed to take forever to save up enough. I remember Tim Murdoch and John Paine coming over to Takapuna and they had great looking boards.'*

Wayne started going on surf trips with Tim and John, and Peter Way. They would frequently stay in the 'Sands Hotel' (sleep on the beach) at Whangamata. *'We were so at home there that one morning, when the surf life saving patrol came along the beach in their Land Rover and told us to clean up the mess on the sand dunes, one of the boys replied, "Get your f***ing Land Rover out of my kitchen".'*

Wayne entered his first nationals at New Plymouth in 1965 and won the junior section. The following year, at Gisborne, he won the first of five senior titles in a row (1966-70). Initially, Wayne viewed the nationals as a social event and a chance to catch up with fellow surfers from around the country. The competitive aspect was not too important. As the years rolled by, however, it became more important to do well in the contests – he wanted to go to the world championships in California (1966) and Puerto Rico (1968) and join the national team

PHOTO TIM MURDOCH

(above) Wayne at Waitara, New Plymouth, 1968 - new board and new moves.

(right) Wayne showing the type of moves that kept him champion from Malibu to short board.

PHOTO TIM MURDOCH

PHOTO BOB COMER

From the ankle-slappers at Takapuna Beach, Auckland **(left)**, to the power of Sunset Beach, Hawaii, 1967 **(below)**, Wayne showed his ability and poise in all conditions.

PHOTO TIM MURDOCH

(above) **Wayne in James Dean mode on a surf trip to Great Barrier Island, 1967.**

travelling to Australia. *'Contest success was a good way to get free trips.'*

When Wayne began working for Atlas Woods, competition success was also important for maintaining his profile as a board builder. More contest success meant more board sales and a better lifestyle. Atlas Woods wanted to stay at number one and they wanted the number one surfer on their team. However, after his 1970 victory at the nationals, Wayne declared himself finished with competition surfing and never went back to it.

Much more important to Wayne was his developing career as a shaper. He got his first start in shaping when Peter Way tossed him two-thirds of a broken blank and told him to 'have a go at that'. Wayne did have a go and shaped a 6'6" board when the norm for the time was about 9'. He surfed it but found it too

hard compared to the 9' board so he sold it to Steve King's brother, Paul. After that, Wayne started doing ding repair work in Takapuna and would fix the boards of his local heroes. They were very encouraging and if he asked for £5 for the job, they would give him £10.

Wayne met Bob McTavish during a 1966 trip to Hawaii, California and Australia. McTavish was one of Australia's leading shapers at that time and he took the young Wayne Parkes under his wing. *'He ran me through shaping a board at the Cord factory in Sydney, which was one of the best at the time.'* On his return to New Zealand, Wayne landed a job at Atlas Woods and worked at the Wairau Road factory as surfer, board designer and shaper of his own signature model. There were also a lot of surf trips in the Land Rover owned by Jacky Mitchell, daughter of Alan Mitchell who owned Atlas Woods. The Land Rover would be piled high with boards and surfers and taken off to remote locations for prolonged periods of time when everyone was supposed to be working.

The following year (1967), Wayne went to Sydney again and enjoyed another big learning experience with McTavish. *'There was a huge amount of experimentation going on with the shape and length of boards, and with the psychedelic stuff. I remember regular visits to the factory by Nat Young and Peter Drouyn. Besides them, I was working alongside George Greenough, Russell Hughes, Kevin Platt and Algie Grudd.'*

McTavish had sufficient confidence in Wayne to leave him to finish off shaping his boards while he went surfing. Wayne would spend the New Zealand winter in Sydney, then return to Auckland for summer and put all his new found experience to work at Atlas Woods. *'I had seven straight years of summer by working that way, and plenty of good surf.'*

Wayne has continued his career as a successful shaper right up to the present day. He has been described by his peers as aloof, inspiring, tough, a smart-arse and the best. He remains one of the most well known surfers in New Zealand and arguably our most successful domestic champion.

(below) **Wayne executing a good bottom turn at Whangamata, 1968.** Don Prince: *'I got my first board when I was 15 after saving the proceeds of a summer's whitebaiting off the Devonport wharf. Most of my friends had them by then and we had a good big group who surfed at Takapuna. We had enough people for games of rugby on the beach at low tide which were always fairly vigorous – face rubs and dumpings by tough-guy Wayne Parkes were common. He was the surf hero at Takapuna and dominated on water and land.'*

sponsors happy (an issue that is still raised today). Elizabeth McDermott recalls John griping about this very problem just prior to his retiring from competition. Following the 1968 nationals, Taff Kennings wrote in 'Surfing with the Star' (a weekly column in the *Auckland Star* newspaper) that there were too many judges with commercial interests who were favouring their team riders and prospects.

Doug Hislop surfed in the nationals, as a senior, from 1967-1971. *'The results would often depend on who the judges were. I tried reasonably hard and got into the New Zealand team to compete for the "Tasman Bucket". I also made the team for the world champs in Puerto Rico but I couldn't afford to go so Ronnie Roman, who was travelling over there at the time, took my place.'*

Chris Ransley was second to Alan Byrne in the juniors and won the Del International Trophy at the 1968 nationals at Christchurch. *'I was a keen competitor and there was quite strong competition to make the Gisborne regional team for the nationals. I beat Al Byrne a few times in the local competitions but Alan always won the important ones, except the Del at Christchurch in 1968. For the Del, I beat Wayne and Alan who were almost invincible in those days. There was a definite tendency for the sponsored surfers to do well in the competitions – they already had two points on you before you hit the water.'*

Alan Byrne: *'Yeah, that was probably true but I didn't mind because I was on the receiving end of it. That sort of stuff has always gone on with the contests and still does today.'*

The Del International Trophy was introduced to the nationals by Nigel Dwyer in 1967 to try and circumvent some of the arguments about who was really the 'best' surfer but it was still a competition amongst those who had already made it through the ranks.

Morale declined a little further with the 1969 nationals being held in poor surf at New Plymouth. A proposal was even put forward to run the nationals at Gisborne every year because of the abundance of surf, accommodation and audience facilities. The idea was dropped because of the advantage to local surfers.

Alan Byrne (*top left*), **Chris Ransley** (*above*) and **Doug Hislop** (*left*) were all strong contest surfers but acknowledged that the results on any given day could depend on who the judges were and whether a surfer was considered a favourite.

Peter Fitzsimmons: *'The nationals hit a low point in 1972 at Westport when they were cancelled due to poor surf. There was a real sense of resentment around and I felt that surfing had really lost some if its soul around that time. That's when I got out for a while.'*

The nationals found a place in surfing life but it was always going to be for a select few who had the skills and inclination to compete. The rewards were there for those who succeeded – trips overseas, glory and potential earnings in the surf industry – but for most surfers the national surf championships were just a sideshow to the sport they loved.

(right) The Quane Trophy on the day it left Gisborne for the Windansea trophy cabinet.

(below) Mid-Shore Board Riders Club, of Christchurch, at the 1964 nationals. The influence of the Californian club scene is evident in the printed team shirts.

Interclub competition

In the same way that the nationals was first run in order to get the country's isolated surfers together, interclub competitions began, as soon as clubs were formed, in order to keep up the contacts made at the nationals. Everyone enjoyed an excuse to get together, surf and have a party afterwards. There were regular contests between the clubs and within the clubs themselves.

This interclub rivalry was acknowledged by Denis Quane when he introduced the Quane Trophy to the 1966 nationals at Gisborne. The trophy was for the team who accumulated the most points at the 1966 nationals, and on a challenge basis thereafter. Gisborne Board Riders was the successful club and they soon had to defend it against Bay Surfers (a second club from Mount Maunganui in which Bob Davie was team leader).

The Quane Trophy made for successful and exciting competition amongst the clubs and the trophy changed hands many times over the next two years. (The rules for the challenges were as follows: five judges who stayed the same throughout the challenge and included one from each club and three independents; there was a minimum of 10 and a maximum 18 surfers allowed in each team; there were no divisions; the five best rides were counted; totals were added to get a winner. If a club challenged and lost, it couldn't challenge again until the trophy changed hands.) Bay Surfers won the trophy from Gisborne Board Riders in the winter of 1966, and subsequently defended it successfully against Surf Syndicate, Whangamata and Point Board Riders. North Reef appear to have won it then before losing it again to Gisborne Board Riders.

Windansea

When Wayne Parkes, Alan Byrne and Dave Burns attended the 1966 World Surfing Championship at San Diego they met Thor Svensen, the president of the Windansea surf club. Alan Byrne: *'He was looking to globalise the club and asked if we would like to join the club and start a branch in New Zealand. It was such an honour for a 15-year-old from Gisborne. When we got back, the*

Auckland guys got things underway and I just cruised along with it, not really thinking about it that much, and, at 15, certainly not worrying about the politics of it.'

The Windansea club made a visit to New Zealand in 1967 bringing some of the stars of the club along – Skip Frye, Mike Purpus (current US champion in 1967), Steve Bigler, Joey Hamasaki and Margo Godfrey. John Paine had the job of chaperone and he took them around the country for five days. They drove 1300 miles searching for surf but had little luck. Their presence was met with a mixture of awe and surprise.

Peter Morse: *'It was pretty amazing to have such big names arriving in town. We didn't get to see them surf but their mere presence seemed to connect us to the rest of the surfing world.'*

Chris Ransley: *'When the Windansea team visited Gisborne, they seemed to be riding old boards and have old styles – stuck in a California time warp.'*

The visit by Windansea really kicked off the affiliated club in Auckland and they attracted the best of New Zealand's surfers to a 30-strong exclusive club. With a team that included Wayne Parkes, Alan Byrne, Peter Way, Doug Hislop, Taff Kennings, Andy McAlpine, Steve King, Bruce Blanchard, Tony Ogilvy, Don Prince, Peter Calder, Dave Allison, Graham Gantley, Jim Carney, Robbie Bambury and Dave Carter, there was little hope for the other clubs in New Zealand.

Dave Rees-George was president of North Reef Board Club from whom most of the Windansea members came. *'Clubs needed their elite surfers to keep it interesting for the others and to act as mentors for new surfers. North Reef eventually dispersed to Windansea for the top riders and Hope Ranch for those left over.'*

Windansea challenged Gisborne for the Quane Trophy in 1968 and won easily. There were a few challenges for Windansea after that but they had secured the services of so many of the top surfers that the challenging clubs were easily disposed of and the challenges stopped coming. Steve King wrote in 1968, in the first edition of *Surfing New Zealand*, *'It [Windansea] has brought together a close-knit group of good surfers whose aim is to get New*

PHOTO GEOFF LOGAN, PHOTO NEWS

(above) The Windansea team, with the Quane Trophy, after their victory over Gisborne Board Riders, 1968. A who's who of New Zealand's top contest surfers: (l to r, standing) Peter Way, Doug Hislop, Dave Carter, Robbie Bambury, Taff Kennings, Alan Byrne, Bruce Blanchard, Steve King, Jim Carney, Neville Seaward, (l to r, sitting) Steven Massey, Wayne Parkes, Peter Tremaine.

Zealand surfing on an international level ... Although people think Windansea is a glory seeking, win or bust club, it is in fact helping other clubs to help themselves, by offering a great challenge which someday may be met ...'

There seemed to be a definite 'air' to Windansea and they were not afraid to revel in their victory over Gisborne. Chris Ransley, who had declined an offer to join Windansea after his Del International victory at the 1968 nationals, was particularly mentioned in the post-challenge media reports. In 'Surfing with the Star' Chris' performance was described as follows: *'... shock winner of last month's Del International – didn't impress anyone. Maybe you get weary of his style which is uncoordinated and jerky ...'.* The challenge to topple Windansea was not taken up and the big imbalance created by Windansea's exclusive team brought about an end to interclub challenges for the Quane Trophy.

(right, l to r) Surf Syndicate members, Pete Cogan, Glen Kelly, Graeme Bambury, Dave Carter and Robbie Bambury. Surf Syndicate were a breakaway club that formed in 1966. They had an invitation-only membership and were, in this respect, a precursor to Windansea. They actually got a reputation for their excesses while on surf trips as much as for their contest results. In February 1967, the club was suspended from the NZSRA, and banned from 1967 Gisborne nationals, for alleged 'unbecoming behaviour'.

PHOTO TAFF KENNINGS COLLECTION

(below) The Mount Board Riders' Club would charter a bus to go to Gisborne for inter-club competitions, checking any suitable surf spots along the way. There would be up to 40 people, their boards and plenty of liquid refreshments. Ted Davidson: 'Our bus had to stop in the Waioeka Gorge one time because of a slip. It was midnight and freezing so we all did 'The Stomp' to stay warm. That story made the local paper.'

PHOTO DAVE WALPOLE

But wait, there's more ...

Contest surfing continued to be quite popular during the mid-60s. Aside from the nationals and the Quane Trophy, local clubs ran open contests – for example, Point Board Riders held an open contest at Whangamata and North Reef held an open contest at Waipu. The contests were organised as club events but anyone could enter, hence they were 'open'. These contests were seen as a good opportunity for younger members of the clubs to surf against the more experienced senior members.

After overtures from the NZSRA, the Australian association agreed to an annual trans-Tasman contest for a trophy that was poetically named the Tasman Bucket. The Australians competed as state teams and the first Tasman Bucket, held at Manly Beach in 1968, was won by New South Wales. The contest was organised at the very last moment at the Australian end, to the point of there being no one to meet the New Zealand team at the airport. After a scramble, the team of Bob Davie, Taff Kennings, Wayne Parkes, Alan Byrne, Doug Hislop and manager Peter Fitzsimmons was finally greeted by the Aussies (see photo on page 80).

Team selection for the Tasman Bucket seemed to contain some of the same intrigue that was encroaching on the rest of competitive surfing in New Zealand at the time. Chris Ransley: *'I wasn't even invited to the trials for the Tasman Bucket even though I was the current Del International champ – the Del cup says "Awarded to the best overall surfer of 1967-68". There was a particular 'cartel' who were running the selection process and I was on the outer. In fact the Gisborne club as a whole was on the outer – we didn't have a good representation in the NZSRA and I didn't have anyone pushing my case.'* Despite missing out on the team, Chris went on to win the junior and open paddleboard sections at the 1969 nationals at New Plymouth. He also received the Catalina Cup for the surfer who accumulated the most points for the 1969 nationals.

A second Tasman Bucket contest was arranged for New Plymouth in January 1969 but it never eventuated due to lack of interest from the Australians.

First to see the light?

On New Zealand's east coast, Gisborne is the first place in the world to see the sun rise each morning. In the mid- to late 60s, Gisborne was considered by many to be the Mecca for surfing. After the pioneering work of Dave Swan, John Logan, Kevin Pritchard and company, a strong young crew of surfers began to emerge, making Gisborne Board Riders one of the strongest clubs in the country. They enjoyed an abundance of waves and breaks, and there was plenty of international input into the Gisborne area.

Bob Davie ensured that some of the country's best board building was occurring in the city, and there was a steady flow of Australians and Americans passing through to inspire the local surfers. The visitors introduced a lot of the alternative culture that was developing in their home countries – new music, clothes and drugs often arrived in Gisborne before the rest of New Zealand. (Mickey Dora, of Malibu fame, spent time in Gisborne before being arrested while trying to flee from creditors.)

Chris Ransley started surfing in 1962 with contemporaries Alan and Terry Byrne, Glen Sutton and Billy Goodwin. *'There were only about 30 surfers in all in our crew. The "old guys" were about 19-20 years old and had cars – having a car made you a king. The main mode of transport for the younger guys was pushbike which was OK because surfing at the end of the road was best anyway – there were no crowds and plenty of waves, and we could leave our board in the front yards of the people who lived on the beach. Our standard of surfing rose quite quickly with Alan Byrne, Billy Goodwin and myself out in empty waves.*

'We would surf before and after school, building a fire on the beach first because we had no wetsuits.

'I got my car licence in 1965 and that opened up a world of possibilities. Surfing at Makarori and Wainui became a regular event, and we explored Mahia and East Cape, being among the first to surf these places. We did plenty of miles, got up to plenty of

(above) **Gisborne was a magnet for surfers because of abundant waves, good lifestyle and a strong surf club.**

(right, l to r) **Gail Patty and Bob Davie formed the backbone of Gisborne Board Riders and made it one of the best surf riders' clubs in the country.**

PHOTO GEOFF LOGAN, PHOTO NEWS

PHOTO GRAY CLAPHAM COLLECTION

(left) **Gisborne Board Riders juniors at an open club contest, Waikanae Beach, 1965. (l to r) Kevin Lewis, Alan Byrne, Howard Brangwin, Denzil Owen and Barry Robinson.**

(above) John McDermott at Waikanae Beach, Gisborne 1966. John was one of many Australians attracted to the charms of Gisborne.

(above) The view of Sponge Bay, from 1965, showing what an enjoyable wave it can be.

(left) Bob Comer and friends, on a 1966 expedition to Gisborne, visiting Sponge Bay.

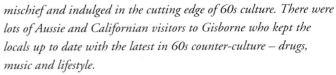

mischief and indulged in the cutting edge of 60s culture. There were lots of Aussie and Californian visitors to Gisborne who kept the locals up to date with the latest in 60s counter-culture – drugs, music and lifestyle.

'Bob McTavish was doing some pretty interesting work when he came to Gisborne to shape at Bob Davies Surfboards. It was just before he got into the shortboards. There was quite a bit of experimentation going on while he was here. Bob Davie was right up with the times and producing cutting edge boards.'

Geoff Logan was a Gisborne surfer who took up the sport in 1964. He grew up working on his father's magazine, *Photo News*. *'I could work in the darkroom and on the magazine production at night, and surf during the day – perfect for a young grommet. I made sure that surfing stayed in the news and got as many shots as possible of my mates – Glen Sutton, Ian (Proto) Steed, Barry and John Robinson, Greg Warren, Mark Jones, Alan Murphy, Spotty Henderson, Denzil Owen, Ron Ammam, Jim Croskery and Wayne (Smokey) Fairlie. I got involved with the Gisborne Board Riders and became president in 1969-70. I initiated some community projects to improve our image, such as collecting for a charity and tidying up a local playground. I would then put some pictures of our efforts in* Photo News *and suddenly local sponsors were easier to find.'*

Gray Clapham was a third-former in 1967. He began surfing with Billy Raggatt, Brent Simpson, Victor Jacobs, Murray Lecompte and Wayne Birrell. *'We were the grommets to the first generation of surfers such as Ian Steed, Alan Byrne, Geoff Logan and John Robinson. They had a big, white Chevy they zoomed around in and they seemed to always be going to parties and hanging out with girls. We aspired to their status and having a car. We were surfing the first real wave of second hand boards such as Bob Davie and Atlas Woods. We were also straight in on the first of the short boards. I had a 7'6" Hannah with a paisley bottom. Wayne "Smokey" Fairlie made his own short board around this time, six-footish, and met with derision but he was just ahead of his time. Lots of Malibus were just hacked down to make shortboards.*

continued on page 109

Alan Byrne

Alan made a big impression on surfing in the 60s despite only being a teenager. John Logan remembers first seeing Alan at a surf contest organised at Waikanae. *'I had heard about Alan but I got a shock when he arrived and cleaned us all up at the ripe old age of about 12.'*

Alan is one of our most successful domestic and international competitors but the thing he liked most about competing was the opportunity to ride great surf locations with six or fewer surfers out. (Alan has four national junior board riding titles, four junior paddle titles and three senior titles. He has placed second in the Pipe Masters in Hawaii and reached the top 20 in the world after one particularly successful year.) His competitive record would have tempted many to try a life of professional competition but Alan found he could travel and live just as comfortably in the more satisfying career of shaping.

He first started surfing in 1962 after his father, Des, made him a 7' board. *'Dad was a real old-style handy man. He built surf skis from* Popular Mechanics *and after he saw his first Malibu boards at a surf life saving carnival in Gisborne, he went to the Condorcraft factory and just built one from what he had seen. He thought it would be good for taking out the set lines we used for fishing. He built one for my brother Terry as well.'*

Alan surfed all of Waikanae Beach with Terry, Glen Sutton, Bob Clay, Barry Broughton, Kevin Pritchard, Dave Burns and Denzil Owen, amongst others. He was also involved with the Waikanae Surf Life Saving Club but that ended up taking a back seat to his new passion for surfing.

'My parents said I was too young to surf Makarori when I was 12 but Terry was allowed to. I used to bike out and watch him. When Mum and Dad finally agreed to let me surf there, I went out with Terry and it was five-footish and only the two of us out. Mum and Dad drove out to watch but they freaked out when I came off and I was swimming around trying to body surf in and retrieve my

board. They banned me from Makarori and that ban has never been lifted. I used to go out anyway and I had a signal system with my friends in case my parents turned up. I would sit out the back and wait for the all clear.'

Alan was only 13 years old when the 1964 nationals were held. Bob Davie had offered to take him up but his parents chose to take him along. He was a surprise winner in the junior section, beating Wayne Parkes and winning an Atlas Woods surfboard. *'Peter Way said he would shape me a custom board and swap it for the Atlas. But Bob wanted to shape my boards so I swapped the Peter Way for a new board from Bob and he did all my boards after that.'* Bob Davie was mentor and patron to the young Alan Byrne. *'Bob and Nigel Dwyer were like father figures for me. They were great surfers and party animals. They would get me drunk and disorderly but in a fun way.'*

The morning that Alan saw Chip Post out surfing at Gisborne was a turning point in his surfing psyche. *'I was out surfing and I looked down the beach at this guy taking off on a wave and he just ran up to the nose and back, cut back, went switch foot, came off the top, and I was just so amazed. I paddled straight in*

(top) **Alan showing the power and style that took him to the top as a contest surfer. His board in this photo is typical of the transition period between the long and short boards at the end of the 60s.**

(above) **Alan as a 13-year-old, competing in the first club champs for Gisborne Board Riders.**

(*above*) **Alan displays the spoils of a successful nationals, Gisborne, 1967.**

(*below*) **Alan Byrne at home, surfing Centres at Makarori Beach, Gisborne, 1971.**

and sat on the beach and watched him. There were lots of us just sitting there watching. That one morning made all the difference for me.' Alan had also heard about the Auckland surfers but had not seen them until one day when Wayne Parkes, Robbie and Graham Bambury, and Steve King turned up at Makarori. *'They looked so heavy. Wayne had a black board and they were all quite a way ahead of us with their surfing – about 18 months I thought. I was in awe of Wayne and never really saw him as a rival. He had a well deserved reputation and was the king. He looked after me at the worlds and introduced me to Nat and some my other heroes which was just unbelievable. He also got me into a reasonable amount of trouble.'*

In 1966, the first New Zealand surfing team to compete overseas went to the world champs at San Diego. The team consisted of Alan, Wayne Parkes and Dave Burns (judge and chaperone from Gisborne). Alan flew to Auckland and was amazed at its size – Los Angeles was even more astounding for him. *'The travel and mixing with the surf heroes of the time was just mind boggling for a 15-year-old from Gisborne.'*

Only the senior champion (Wayne Parkes) was sent to the 1968 world champs in Puerto Rico but Bob Davie shouted Alan (the junior champion) the fare, confident of his abilities to surf at the highest level. Wayne lent Alan a board after his was stolen while in Puerto Rico and Alan went on to make the semi-finals and ninth place overall on the borrowed board. *'While I was at the world champs I met Reno Abellira and David Nuuhiwa who sort of took me under their wings. After the worlds, I went with them to the Virgin Islands and LA. I drove around LA in a Porsche with Reno and David who was like the king of surfing at that time. It was wild.'*

Back in Gisborne, Alan was getting old enough to go on surf trips. *'I did a lot of trips with Terry and Glen Sutton, and we would go to Mahia and the Mount but not much outside of Gisborne. I never even surfed Raglan until the late 60s. The Whangamata bar was a favourite of mine. I got lots of waves there.'*

At the end of 1967, Alan was due to finish school so Bob Davie offered him a job learning to shape at his factory at Mount Maunganui. Alan had spent quite a bit of time in Bob's factory at Gisborne and knew about building boards. Bob also offered Des Byrne a job as factory manager and glasser so the whole family packed up and left for Mount Maunganui in 1968. After the summer of 68-69, Alan left for a period of overseas exploration and adventure. He returned off and on after that for summer shaping contracts and to surf in the nationals but he spent a significant amount of time touring the world as surfer and shaper.

By 1973 Alan had gotten a bit sick of surfing and shaping so he joined the airforce and trained as air crew. After watching the moon landings he had an urge to become an astronaut and felt the airforce was the first step to getting into space. However, the airforce stopped teaching him new things by 1976 so he dropped out and found himself back in the surfing industry. Today, Alan is living in Queensland and still shaping, surfing, travelling and helping to raise his three children.

'The more boards you could get on a car the better – it showed you had lots of friends. It was also a matter of few cars and lots of surfers. I remember Gisborne being a Mecca for Aussies for a while. They brought the drug and surfing culture to Gisborne, and big parties and wild flats.'

Doug Hislop: 'I moved to Gisborne in 1966 because it was THE place to surf at the time. I was a beach agent for Del Surfboards but didn't push it too much because I knew that Bob and Nigel were mates. I kept a surf diary during my time in Gisborne which shows what the surf was like, where I surfed and who I was surfing with. There were a lot of Aussies coming through town at that stage and they really gave everyone a hurry up on the surfing. It was a great time to be in Gisborne.'

PHOTO TIM MURDOCH

(left) Gisborne has produced one of New Zealand's supreme contest surfers and shapers in Alan Byrne. Here he is shown surfing at Makarori Centres, 1971. Alan was a very successful convert to the new shortboard designs and the style required to surf them.

(below) Gisborne was also an important testing ground for Wayne Parkes, and he won two national titles there.

PHOTO GEOFF LOGAN, PHOTO NEWS

(above) Doug Hislop, Gisborne, 1967. Peter Tremaine: 'Coming back from the '68 Christchurch nationals there was a running battle between Doug Hislop's car and Peter Way's. There were eggs and bottles flying, and buckets of indescribably disgusting goo. Ambushes would be laid on one-way bridges and around sharp corners. The cars were caked and disgusting when we pulled into Gisborne. The grand finale was Doug getting stopped by a cop because his car looked so foul.'

PHOTO RICK BRADLEY

The popularity of surfing New Plymouth at the end of the 60s was reinforced by the nationals being held there three years running, 1969-71.
(right) Wayne Parkes in training on a small day at Weld Road, New Plymouth, 1968.

(below) A photo that gives an indication of the size and intensity for which Taranaki surf was well known, Opunake, 1963.

PHOTO TIM MURDOCH

PHOTO MIKE GARDINER

(below) Unknown surfers at East End Beach, New Plymouth, 1968. The wealth of breaks and consistent swell made Taranaki a popular surf destination during the late 60s.

PHOTO NEIL REID

The Wild West

On the other side of the North Island, where the sun sets, Taranaki was beginning to attract more and more visitors due to its consistent waves and abundance of reefs and points. The magnetic personality of Nigel Dwyer also attracted surfers to New Plymouth for the parties! If Gisborne was the home of surfing in the mid- to late 60s, Taranaki was the place to go in the late 60s to early 70s. Peter Way: *'New Plymouth is world class for surf – it's just a pity about the temperature. I spent a few years there surfing in Wonderland – so many good breaks.'*

Doug Hislop moved back to New Plymouth in 1968 and worked for Nigel Dwyer as a glasser. *'I travelled all over the country surfing. I owned a 36 Chevy when I was in Gisborne and I would drive over to Taranaki for a weekend's surfing – five or six hours' driving – and I sometimes did that three weekends in a row! I remember one weekend when I was driving over with Billy Goodwin and it was pouring all the way. The windscreen wipers weren't working so Billy was under the dash pulling them back and forth, by hand, all the way over.*

'Nigel and I discovered a lot of spots around Taranaki but I particularly remember the day we drove a Land Rover along Stent Road and over some farm land to discover that famous break. It was too obvious to call it Stent Road so we referred to it as Rover Point for a while but word soon got out.'

New Plymouth required reasonable ability in the water because of the size of the surf – this would deter many and attract some. No legropes meant that surfers had to be able to manage the swim or stick to beaches they could manage. (Losing boards in the surf meant there was always more room in the line-up. The advent of legropes has increased crowding for that reason alone.)

Wayne Arthur is a true pioneer of surfing in Taranaki and a member of the 'Brady Brigade'. *'There was a bunch of us that got attracted to the mighty Bradford, a two-cylinder, wood-framed, aluminium-bodied van that we could sleep in. The Brady Brigade used to take off about midnight, with a skin full of piss, and hit the*

*coast south to Opunake or north to Awakino, and beyond, depend-
ing on the forecast. It was totally irresponsible, playing demolition
derby all the way there but there were no major accidents or mishaps
other than boards flying off the roof racks. The Bradies could only get
to around 50mph so no real damage could be done.*

*'Competitive surfing was a part of the culture, more for the parties
than the dreams of success for me personally. It was a good way to meet
other surfers from around the country. Overseas surfers were treated
like real guests of honour and another good excuse for a party. We
assumed they had to be better surfers than us but looking back, they
weren't any better than guys like Wayne Parkes and Alan Byrne.*

*'The whole Taranaki Coast was open to being discovered. Some of
the spots were too hostile to start with – with no legropes, the prospect
of damage was very real. As each new spot got discovered, we would
pounce on it and surf it almost exclusively until another spot found
favour. When legropes came in [1970s], the whole coast came alive.'*

Gerald Turner was becoming enthusiastic about sailing in
1963 when he saw his first surfboard at Red Beach, north of
Auckland. His dad asked if he would like a surfboard instead of a
yacht. Gerald tried to make his own board at first, using insulation foam, but he neglected to use a protective coat over the
foam and the board broke in half after only two or three waves.

Gerald saved money from forestry work and bought a Peter
Byers board from Dave Littlejohn. A steady flow of visiting surfers
including Peter Ray, Terry Tumeth and Alan Dorman helped
inspire Gerald, as did local surfers such as Robert Wagstaff, Ray
Priest, Tommy Waite, John Bonas, Peter Quinn, Leith
Beaurepaire, Wayne Arthur, Roger Hobbs and Larry Wilkie.

*'I won the Taranaki regional champs and, after moving to
Wellington for work, won the Wellington champs twice. I had a
good natured rivalry going with Paddy Perkinson. I also managed a
third in the 1966 nationals.*

*'I used to learn moves from the magazines and any movies that
came through and then go and try them out in the water.'*

Don Prince, an Auckland grommet in the late 60s, recalls a
trip to New Plymouth with Peter Tremaine. *'We caught the train*

PHOTO DAVE LITTLEJOHN

(left) **The camping ground at Fitzroy Beach
in the foreground and a sample of the
waves for which New Plymouth was
renowned in the background. Lyn
Humphreys:** *'I have lots of fond memories of
those times – camping at Fitzroy during the
nationals with so many surfers around and
everyone buzzing, stomps at the Opunake Hall,
especially when Aussie surfers passed through
on "surfari", and huddled around the fire with
a big group of friends on a cold winter's
morning at Waiwhakaiho after some great
waves.'*

(below) **The men's finalists of the 1969 nationals at New Plymouth
head for the water. The photo gives a great view of where board
design was up to in 1969 – shorter and sharper. *(l to r)* Doug Hislop,
Taff Kennings, Wayne Parkes, Alan Byrne, Mike Court (obscured) and
Mike Tinkler. Wayne went on to win his fourth consecutive title.**

PHOTO GEOFF LOGAN, PHOTO NEWS

(right) Second Point, White Rock, Wairarapa Coast, 1971. The Wairarapa Coast was a popular destination for the Wellington surfers when they went looking for waves.

(below) Mike Draffin, Cape Palliser, Wairarapa Coast, 1971.

PHOTO MIKE McGLYNN

PHOTO MIKE McGLYNN

(below) Saint Clair, Dunedin, 1965. Ted Davidson: 'On one trip to Dunedin, I went surfing at huge Saint Clair in an unofficial one-on-one competition with Bart Smaill. I didn't really want to go out because of the size but did so in the interests of board sales to the local surfers who were eagerly watching us. I got a lucky break paddling out and managed to get out the back without too much trouble. However, the surf was huge and I was pretty scared so I caught one wave and came straight in, happy to concede to Bart and still be alive. A couple of guys got washed up on the rocks that day and took quite a beating.'

PHOTO NEIL REID

down during school holidays and stayed with Nigel [Dwyer]. He gave us non-stop abuse for being kiwi bludgers and anything else he could think of but he let us sleep in his garage and organised rides to the surf for us every day – just his way of making us feel welcome. It was a bit like the Wild West down there. Robbie Walsh and Robin Bull called me in Auckland one day to say they were coming up for the weekend. They hadn't really been out of New Plymouth much so they were quite amped up. Unfortunately, rumour has it they hired a mini-tanker of beer, hooked it up to the Chevy and took hoses in through the back window. Apparently, they crashed at Waitara and never made it to Auckland. I never found out how true that was.'

I'll leave the last word on the Wild West to Larry Keating, a frequent visitor to New Plymouth during the 60s: 'A group of us Wellingtonians were invited to a house wrecking party somewhere around Hawera. Apparently, a farmer wanted a house removed and was going to burn it down the next day. We were given an address and told to get there with a dozen flagons of beer and a hatchet each. We got there at about 7pm. It was dark and the lads who had invited us hadn't arrived, so we got on with hacking and smashing the house. Finally, we thought we might as well do what the farmer intended and set the thing on fire. What a blaze! Pissed and yahooing we watched in amazement as the flames engulfed the old villa. Two hours after arriving our mates had still not turned up so we decided to head back to New Plymouth. About five miles down the road, there were the guys, four or five car loads, with headlights beamed on a house, and they were ripping into this place with sledge hammers and axes. WE HAD BURNED DOWN THE WRONG HOUSE! Needless to say, we headed for Wellington in great haste. I never did hear the outcome of that.'

Wellington has waves?

Wellington tended to be overlooked as a surf location despite supporting a large population of surfers. One reason was that Welllington's board riders actually came from specific areas such as Titahi Bay, Hutt Valley and the town beaches, and they tended to travel outside Wellington to favourite breaks on the Kapiti and Wairarapa Coasts. Riders from Wellington were a common sight around New Plymouth.

New young riders such as Mike McGlynn, Peter Furze, Gary McCormick and Mike Draffin were leading the charge to breaks like Castle Point, Ning Nong and Plimmerton. Other local standouts, Groob (Fat Cat Surfboards) and Roger Titcombe (Roger Titcombe Surfboards), went on to open board shops in the early 70s following the trend to local, custom board building.

This appears to have been the first time that boards were being built in Wellington since the departure of Jim Mowtell in 1963. With a wealth of shaping influences from New Zealand's other manufacturers available through Wellington's surf shops (John Conway and Peter Fitzsimmons at Lyall Bay, Peter Miller in the Hutt Valley), Wellington appeared to have no need of a local shaper during the mid to late 60s.

And on the mainland ...

Denis Quane found that his share of the surfboard market was being slowly eroded by the strength of Atlas Woods, Bob Davie and a number of other manufacturers. Denis Quane: *'The only other board builders in the South Island appeared in the late 1960s when boards started to shorten and other material suppliers came on the scene. Jim Tatton was one I can remember. Up until that point, I was supplying pretty much the whole of the South Island and sending boards up to dealers in the North Island.'*

As surfing in the South Island became more popular, surfers such as Dunedin's Brian Laybourne epitomised the expanding pool of surfers that allowed Quane to maintain its strong position. Brian started surfing in 1966 with contemporaries John Leslie (Cog), Brian Munce, Julian Allpress, Brett Sutherland and Bob Franklin. *'We would meet in town on Saturday morning and organise where to go. If anyone was missing, we would leave a note for them. We were still the only ones surfing pretty much anywhere we went. I remember Dave Michaels came from Auckland to Otago*

PHOTO DENIS QUANE

PHOTO ROGER LAND

(above) Quane Surfboards advertisement from 1969 showing where the shapes were going at that time. Denis holding the board.

(left) Unknown surfer at Beatons, near Dunedin, 1970. The speed and manoeuvrability of the new boards meant that many previously unmakeable waves became prime surfing locations.

(above) **Graham Gantley, an apprentice to Takapuna surfers such as Wayne Parkes and Taff Kennings, was one of the grommets of the 60s who became a contest stand-out in the 70s. This photo was taken at Te Arai Point, Northland, 1970.**

University – he was really good and gave everyone a hurry up. There were still very few surfers visiting Dunedin even in 1966. Any piece of information was gobbled up – The Endless Summer was a revelation.'

Brian went on 'surfari' in the North Island during the summer of 1966-67 (stopping at Mount Maunganui to work for Ted Davidson running his board hire business) and then travelled to Australia in 1968 where he was amazed by the standard of surfing. Back in New Zealand, Brian entered the 1968 nationals at Christchurch and remembers the surf being huge in his heat. He joined the South Coast Board Riders Club when it was started by John Leslie and Brett Munce but was not really a competitor – like most surfers he enjoyed the social side of the meetings. The formation of the board riders' club was the first time that there was a division between surfers and surf life savers in Dunedin.

Dunedin pioneer Neil Reid also became a member of the South Coast Board Riders Club but maintained his interest in both surfing and surf life saving, as did most of the originals. Neil spent 1967 working, surfing and surf life saving in Australia. When he returned to Dunedin there was a whole new crop of young surfers in the water who he didn't know and, at the ripe old age of 22, he was called 'grandpa' by one of the young surfers. He knew things had changed.

The outposts still remained, however. Denis Quane: 'Even in the late 60s we would do surf life saving demos over at Westport and there was no surfing going on then. I started sending some boards over in the early 70s but it got off to a very slow start on the West Coast.'

Riding into the next decade ...

The end of the 1960s and arrival of the 1970s heralded a change in surfboard manufacturing with the large factories gradually closing down and being replaced by small local board shops such as Supersession Surfboards in Whangarei, opened in 1970 by Graham Gantley, Graham Allen, Roger Crisp and Dave Leach. The 70s also saw the demise of the 'production' board. Most

surfers wanted a custom-shaped board and preferred to have it shaped by someone who knew the local conditions and the individual's surfing ability. For the first time, there were also enough trained board builders to go out and start the small shops.

Primitive legropes were beginning to appear by the end of the 60s and had a big impact on surfing in the 70s. Where once there was a good turnover of surfers at any break, due to losing boards after falling off and having to swim to retrieve them, now even the less able surfers could immediately get back on their boards and be back in the line-up within a few minutes. Also, legropes meant that a surfer did not necessarily have to be capable of swimming in through surf any more, thus, more people were attracted to try surfing.

Wetsuits were also in common use by the end of the 1960s. This meant that surfers could stay out in cold conditions for a lot longer and crowding of a break was further exacerbated.

And more young surfers, nearly all male, continued to take up the noble sport. The number of surfers probably exceeded 20,000 in 1970, relatively few compared to 1998's estimated 185,000 but still a huge increase over the decade of 1960-70. New names began to appear amongst the contest winners, such as Graham Gantley and Kevin Jarrett.

With a new social climate, new boards and a strong sense of what it was to be a surfer, the new tribe headed into the 1970s with high hopes for peace, love and understanding in the world of surfing. Most of the coastline had been looked over for surf at least once and overseas surf travel had become quite common.

Don Prince: 'Going into the 70s was a time of rapid change and experimentation in all facets of life. What was happening with board design was a metaphor for the times – anything goes. The whole California, hippy, drop out and turn on scene suited the niche that surfing in New Zealand occupied perfectly. Surfers still idolised the USA and Australia and were happy to drop out, surf and get back to nature. Jobs were so easy to come by that dropping out and dropping back in were easy.

'Surfing was a fantastic way to meet people from overseas and the *perfect excuse to travel both locally and internationally. Most people in New Zealand still didn't travel much and had little contact with other countries and their people. Surfers were remarkably cosmopolitan.'*

Graham Gantley, like Don Prince, was a Takapuna Beach local. *'At one stage there were six of us from Takapuna Grammar who were in the Auckland team for the nationals – me, Don Prince, Peter Tremaine, Peter Calder, Tony Ogilvy and one other. We used to make sure we stayed in line or the older guys like Wayne Parkes, Taff Kennings and Steve King would give us a thick ear. They would take us to Piha when we were only 14 years old and too small to get out the back unless it was really small. We made sure we did what those older guys said and gradually learned how to handle the surf. We learned a lot from them.*

'I was asked to be a member of Windansea while I was still at school which was a big thing. It didn't really have that much to do with just going surfing but it was great for the contests. Wayne was my hero back then and I was inspired by his intensity in the surf.' (Graham used that inspiration to achieve third placing in the 1971 nationals, and first placing in the 1972 and 1974 nationals.)

Of the six surfers from Takapuna Grammar who were eligible to go to the 1968 nationals in Christchurch, Graham was the only one refused time off, due to his persistent absence from school to go surfing. He went anyway and was expelled. *'I took the train down with Don Prince. I remember my first heat at 7am at Taylors Mistake – the sand was frozen and crunching under my feet as I walked to the water, and I only had my boardshorts on. Hardly anybody had a wetsuit. Peter Calder got hypothermia and had to go to hospital. We got a ride home with Peter Way – that was the non-stop egg fight from Christchurch to Gisborne against Doug Hislop's car-load.'*

When he returned to Auckland, Graham started with Atlas Woods as a sander before progressing to laminating/finishing, then shaping. He moved to Whangarei in 1970 and started Supersession Surfboards.

In Wellington, Mike McGlynn had returned from a three-year overseas surf trip. *'I found the "summer surfer" influx and the focus on labels was taking the soul out of surfing. Contests were placing individuals on pedestals and it was a bit much for me back then. I headed for the country life, where there was no "surf scene" and worked on starting* Waves *magazine to try and get some soul back into surfing.'*

Surfers returning to their local beaches also found a new crop of young surfers who considered themselves to be the locals. The new generation had respect for the pioneers but no time for the surf life saving roots of surfing. The first generation found that their favourite breaks were getting crowded, and that the big happy family of surfers they had enjoyed through most of the 60s was beginning to include some offspring whose ideas of how to live their lives were quite different from their own. Bob Comer: *'By the end of the 60s I was married and committed to a job and mortgage, as were most of the guys I started surfing with. We didn't have the time or inclination for the drugs and behaviour that the younger guys got into but my board was still always at the ready.'*

(below) Laurie Pinnegar, Raglan, 1969. This photo shows the new speed and lines of attack that were being explored with the shorter boards, particularly in more powerful surf.

PHOTO RICK BRADLEY

Close out

It still comes as a surprise to many young surfers to learn that the origin of surfing was in the surf life saving movement, and that many of the sport's pioneers maintained their interest in surf life saving. Their love and respect for the ocean is what led to their becoming New Zealand's first modern surfers. When Ron White recollects his time surfing at Mount Maunganui's main beach during the mid-1950s – how much he enjoyed sitting out in the water with a couple of friends, in the sunshine, waiting for waves and chatting about this and that – he captures everything that still appeals about surfing in the year 2000. The thrill of enjoying a surf with a few friends remains the biggest motivation for surfers.

Few sports have grown at the pace experienced by surfing during the 60s. Its growth was the result of a curious concoction of science, social change and pioneering spirit. Lightweight surfboards and access to cars resulted in a new social group who were mobile, rowdy and ready to try anything to indulge their new sport.

Despite being an alternative culture in a small country, there was still plenty of money to be made from the surf industry. While the large surfboard manufacturers enjoyed a fruitful decade, they also sowed the seeds of their own demise as they trained more and more board builders who went on to start their own shops. It is another curiosity of surfing that while associated products such as clothing and wetsuits can be manufactured anywhere, surfboards are still shaped to individual needs, for specific waves and locations, by local craftsmen.

I use the word craftsman deliberately because I have not come across any record of women building surfboards during the 60s (or later). Surfing is still dominated by men despite some of our earliest pioneers being women. The physical strength required for surfing was one reason for the dearth of women in the sport but comments from the women surfers indicate that involvement in alternative cultures during the 60s was even less

socially acceptable for them than for males.

The surfing community demonstrated its fringe social status by being in the forefront of the social changes that swept the country in the late 60s, due largely to the influence of foreign surfers in New Zealand and local surfers travelling the world in search of waves. The new philosophy, music, clothes and drugs were already well known to surfers by the time the rest of the country discovered them.

Contest surfing started in New Zealand as an excuse for a social gathering, however, it was always a minority who were involved in the contests and that remains true to this day. The nature of the sport is such that competition is more between the individual and the wave rather than between surfers (once the wave has been caught). The merits and results of contest surfing have always been debated because of the subjective way of judging the sport.

Modern surfing is just over 40 years old in New Zealand, and there have been enormous changes in the sport in that time. The commercial side of surfing is driven by huge sales of clothing and accessories, promoted by increasingly wealthy professional surfers. However, getting out and getting a wave is still the essence of it all.

What will become of surfing with the ever-increasing numbers of people competing for waves has yet to be seen but one visible result is the resurgence of the Malibu board, perfect for catching more waves in crowded and small-wave conditions. However, if you are not going to stay and compete at your local break, travelling to more isolated surf is still an option. I hope that the spirit of exploration will survive ahead of the new threat of ownership and 'rental' of surf breaks as is occurring at some locations in Fiji and Indonesia. There are still a lot of waves around our own coastline that go unridden.

I hope that this book has entertained surfers and non-surfers alike. I believe surfing is still the most enjoyable and challenging sport possible, so remember to make the most of each wave and keep the ocean and beaches clean for those to come.

Epilogue ... or pictures that I loved but couldn't find a place for elsewhere

PHOTO ALAN GODFERY

(above) Ross Edmonson, Pakiri Beach, Northland, 1963.

PHOTO GEOFF LOGAN, PHOTO NEWS

(above, l to r) **Terry Byrne, Peter Goodwin and Roger Jenkins, Makarori Beach, Gisborne, 1964.**

PHOTO RICK BRADLEY

(above) **An unidentified surfer in perfect position – on the nose, on his own.**

(right, l to r) **Bob Atherton and Neville Masters at Shipwreck Bay, Northland, 1964.** *'Neville's tractor was the ideal transport for the beach. It saved us having to carry those heavy boards along the sand.'*

PHOTO BOB & JOAN ATHERTON

(above, l to r) Bob McNabb and Bill Ebdale looking back over Taupo Bay, Northland, 1963.

Some other surfers ...

(above) Paul Von Zalinski, Piha, Auckland, 1963.

(right) Warwick Ross, Pakiri Beach, Northland, 1963.

(below) Rick Bradley, Raglan, 1964.

(above) Mike Styles, Raglan, 1963.

(above) Ray Mead, Whangamata, 1964.

(right) Mike Court, Raglan, 1964. I was unable to interview Mike for this book and subsequently his influence in the text does not parallel the significant influence he had on local surfing. Mike was a strong contest surfer, Raglan pioneer, ex-president of Raglan Board Riders, and retailer/surf entrepreneur from the early 60s through to the present day. The strength of his surfing influenced a whole generation at The Point and Mike can still be seen surfing there today.

(above, l to r) Rod Toohill, Warwick Ross, Bill Ebdale, Unknown, Grant Matheson, Creeth Sidford, Bob McNabb, Geoff Bonham, Shipwreck Bay, Northland, 1963.

PHOTO MIKE GARDINER

(above, l to r) **Ray Cates, Unknown, Ronnie Roman, Mike Gardiner, Unknown, Peter Way, Piha, Auckland, 1959.**

(below) **Daryl Neate, Taylors Mistake, Christchurch, 1963.**

PHOTO ALAN GODFERY

(*above, l to r*) **Bill Ebdale and Ian Crooks, Taupo Bay, Northland, 1963.**

The cars

Talking surfing in the 60s with the originals always ends up incorporating a discussion on what cars they drove. A story will begin with surfing and who was on the trip and quite quickly became an account of what car was used that day and who else was seen in their respective vehicles. These photos give just a hint of the high esteem in which cars were held by the early surfers.

(*below, l to r*) **Campbell Ross, John Greenaway, Graeme Dunne, 'Thomo', Gisborne, 1963.**

(*below*) **Bob Atherton's VW, with son and surfboard, Matauri Bay, Northland, 1966.**

(right) Cars outside the
Raglan Pub after another
session at The Point, 1963.

(below) Bob Comer's Mark I Zephyr with surfboard and fishing rod.

(left) John Paine with his Daimler Dart.
John is sporting a *Surfing Hollow Days*
t-shirt after the visit to New Zealand by
Bruce Brown to film *The Endless Summer.*

PHOTO BOB COMER

PHOTO BOB COMER

PHOTO ALAN GODFERY

Glossary

beach agent A surfer who would take orders at the local beach for a surfboard manufacturer based in a different town, e.g. Del Surfboards was based in New Plymouth but had beach agents at Gisborne, Titahi Bay and Mount Maunganui. The beach agent mailed the order to the manufacturer who made the board and freighted it back. The beach agent received a commission.

blank The base material for a surfboard, such as foam or balsa. The blank was the substrate which was shaped to become a surfboard and subsequently coated with fibreglass and resin to make it strong enough to stand on without snapping but keeping the coat thin enough to retain the qualities of the shaped blank.

broach An old term for turning across the face of the wave in order to ride it. It used to be, on the old longboards, that if your board broached, you could not control the turn and would fall off. The shorter, lighter Malibu boards allowed the turn to be controlled and the face of the wave to be ridden.

custom board Surfboards that were shaped to a specific customer's requirements. The boards would be shaped to take into account the size, ability and style of the surfer, and the type of waves they were surfing. A custom board took longer to shape than a production board and was generally more expensive.

ding Dents, holes or shatters that occur on the surface of a board. Usually the result of collisions with other boards or rocks, or falling off roof racks. Dings need to be fixed so that the foam core of the board doesn't get wet and start to rot.

dropping in The board rider who takes off closest to the breaking part of the wave has right of way. If another surfer takes off further along the unbroken face of the wave and gets in the way of the other surfer, they are said to have 'dropped in'. As surf breaks become more crowded, there is more pressure for waves and surfers may drop in in order to get a ride, resulting in frayed tempers.

gremmie (grommet) This was the name given to the young surfers who were taking up surfing and would hang around the older surfers for inspiration, advice and rides to the surf and parties. All surfers have to go through the gremmie stage as their apprenticeship for surfing.

pintails Where the tail of a booard ends at a point rather than being rounded. A design feature of the late 60s.

pop-out Rather than just making a foam blank inside a mould, the outer fibreglass shell was laid down on each half of the mould so that when the mould was closed up and the foam expanded, the result was a ready-made board with foam sandwiched within a fibreglass shell. All that was required was some sanding.

production board	Surfboards that were shaped to a template with no specific extras. The boards were designed for the 'average' surfer, and catered for the rapid increase in demand for surfboards during the 1960s. Production boards could be made over the winter for the summer market, while custom boards were made during the summer.
rocker	The curve from nose to tail in a board that provides lift in the nose and avoids nose-dives into the waves. Also affects the amount of planing surface on the bottom of the board.
stringer	In order to add strength to boards and try to stop them snapping, foam blanks would be split in half, longways, then glued back together with a thin piece of wood, the stringer, running down the middle. Some boards would have several stringers and they even became a fashion addition to the boards in extreme cases.

Bibliography

Coney, Sandra, *Piha – a history in images*, The Keyhole Press, 1997.

Moran, Kevin, *The Shaping of Aquatics Education in New Zealand Schools*, unpublished MEd. thesis, Massey University, 1999.

Pearson, Kent, *Surfing Subcultures of Australia and New Zealand*, University of Queensland Press, 1979.

Warwick, Wayne, *A Guide to Surfriding in New Zealand*, Viking SevenSeas Ltd, 1978.

(right) **Gail Patty showing 60s style with scooter and board collection.**

PHOTO GAIL PATTY COLLECTION

Thank you all

It has been a real privilege to talk to New Zealand's pioneers of surfing and I thank them for all their assistance and willingness to help me out with this book.

The book would never have made it to publication without the support of my fellow workers at Tradewinds. While I have done the work of writer, researcher and desktop publisher, it is very important to note that the book is a result of the accumulated skills of myself, Matthew, Fraser and Jeannie. I have spent a lot of time on this project and they have covered for me and encouraged me all along the way, and added the vital design and illustration skills that I lack.

I also would never have finished this project without constant support on the home front, encouragement and proofreading from my darling wife, Karen.

Lastly, I would like to apologise to all the surfers who I didn't get to interview, and for all the photos I was unable to include. Perhaps a revised edition will suffice in a couple of years. If anyone wishes to make suggestions or contributions or otherwise, feel free to contact me at *luke@tradewinds.co.nz* or *www.tradewinds.co.nz* or phone (09) 486 6407.

Thank you for assistance above and beyond the call of duty:
Bob Comer, Chas Lake, Mike Gardiner, Gary McCormick for the Foreword, Jeannie Ferguson.

Thank you for vital input and encouragement:
Wayne Arthur, Bob and Joan Atherton, Leith Beaurepaire, Rick Bradley, Murray Bray, Bev Breward, Bruce Brown, Bud Browne, Peter Byers, Alan Byrne, Jock Carson, Gray Clapham, Ken and Lois Clark, Bing Copeland, Frank Cassidy, Bob and Mary Davie, Ted and Mavis Davidson, Rodney Davidson, Taffy Davies, Nigel and Trish Dwyer, Peter Fitzsimmons, Larry Foster, Graham Gantley, John Gisby, Alan Godfery, Ken Griffin, Mike Henry, Doug Hislop, Lyn Humphreys, Dave Jackman, Tony Johnson, Larry Keating, Taff Kennings, Steve King, Roger Land, Brian Laybourne, Dave Littlejohn, Geoff Logan, John Logan, Andy McAlpine, Colin McCoombs, Keith McCulloch, Elizabeth McDermott, Mike McGlynn, Neville and Barbara Masters, Jonette Mead, Peter Miller, Nick Minogue, Alan Mitchell, Brook Mitchell, Jacky Mitchell, Kevin Moran, Peter Morse, Jim Mowtell, Alan Muir, Tim Murdoch, Tim and Mike Newdick, John Paine, Wayne Parkes, Gail Patty, Don Prince, Kevin Pritchard, Max Purdie, Denis Quane, Peter Quinn, Chris Ransley, Neil Reid, Tony Reid, Dave Rees-George, Ron Roman, Campbell Ross, Bart Smaill, David Stork, Dave Swan, Mark Thompson, Peter Tremaine, Gerald Turner, Fred Van Dyke, Dave Walpole, Ron White, Cindy Webb, Peter Way, Bill Walsh, Dale Warwick, Penny Whiting, Frank Wilkin, Roo and Clare Wilson, Tui Wordley.

Thanks also to the non-surfers who helped so generously:
Paul Bateman, Sandra Coney, Wayne Smith (Apple Laser Set), Neil Beattie (BT Scanning). Thanks to Bernice Beachman for giving me a chance and publishing the book.

Every effort has been made to trace the photographers of the many pictures that have come from personal collections. To those whose work has not been credited, or may have been wrongly attributed, the publishers offer an apology.

PENGUIN BOOKS
Penguin Books (NZ) Ltd, cnr Airborne and Rosedale Roads, Albany, Auckland 1310, New Zealand
Penguin Books Ltd, 27 Wrights Lane, London W8 5TZ, England
Penguin Putnam Inc, 375 Hudson Street, New York, NY 10014, United States
Penguin Books Australia Ltd, 487 Maroondah Highway, Ringwood, Australia 3134
Penguin Books Canada Ltd, 10 Alcorn Avenue, Toronto, Ontario, Canada M4V 3B2
Penguin Books (South Africa) Pty Ltd, 5 Watkins Street, Denver Ext 4, 2094, South Africa
Penguin Books India (P) Ltd, 11, Community Centre, Panchsheel Park, New Delhi 110 017, India
Penguin Books Ltd, Registered Offices: Harmondsworth, Middlesex, England

First published by Penguin Books (NZ) Ltd, 2000

1 3 5 7 9 10 8 6 4 2

Copyright © Luke Williamson, 2000

A Tradewinds Publishing concept
Designed and typeset by Tradewinds Publishing, Auckland
Printed by Condor Production, Hong Kong

ISBN 0 14 029890 8